Helen C. Seidlitz Sept 30 '75
Chester Mont

A Mirror for Greatness:
Six Americans

Other books by Bruce Bliven

The Men Who Make the Future
Preview for Tomorrow
The World Changers
Five Million Words Later

As editor

What the Informed Citizen Needs to Know
Twentieth Century Unlimited

A Mirror for Greatness

Six Americans

Bruce Bliven

McGraw-Hill Book Company

New York St. Louis
San Francisco Düsseldorf
Mexico Toronto

Book design by Marcy J. Katz.

123456789MUBP798765

Library of Congress Cataloging in Publication Data

Bliven, Bruce, date
A mirror for greatness.

"Several of the chapters in this book are greatly expanded and rewritten versions of material that has appeared elsewhere."
1. United States—Biography. I. Title.
E176.B59 920'.73 74-22221

ISBN 0-07-005904-7

The author and publisher wish to thank The Sophia Smith Collection (Women's History Archive), Smith College, Northampton, Massachusetts, for permission to include the illustration of Sojourner Truth; also, the New York Public Library Picture Collection for use of the illustrations of Benjamin Franklin, John Adams, Thomas Jefferson, Ralph Waldo Emerson, Henry David Thoreau.

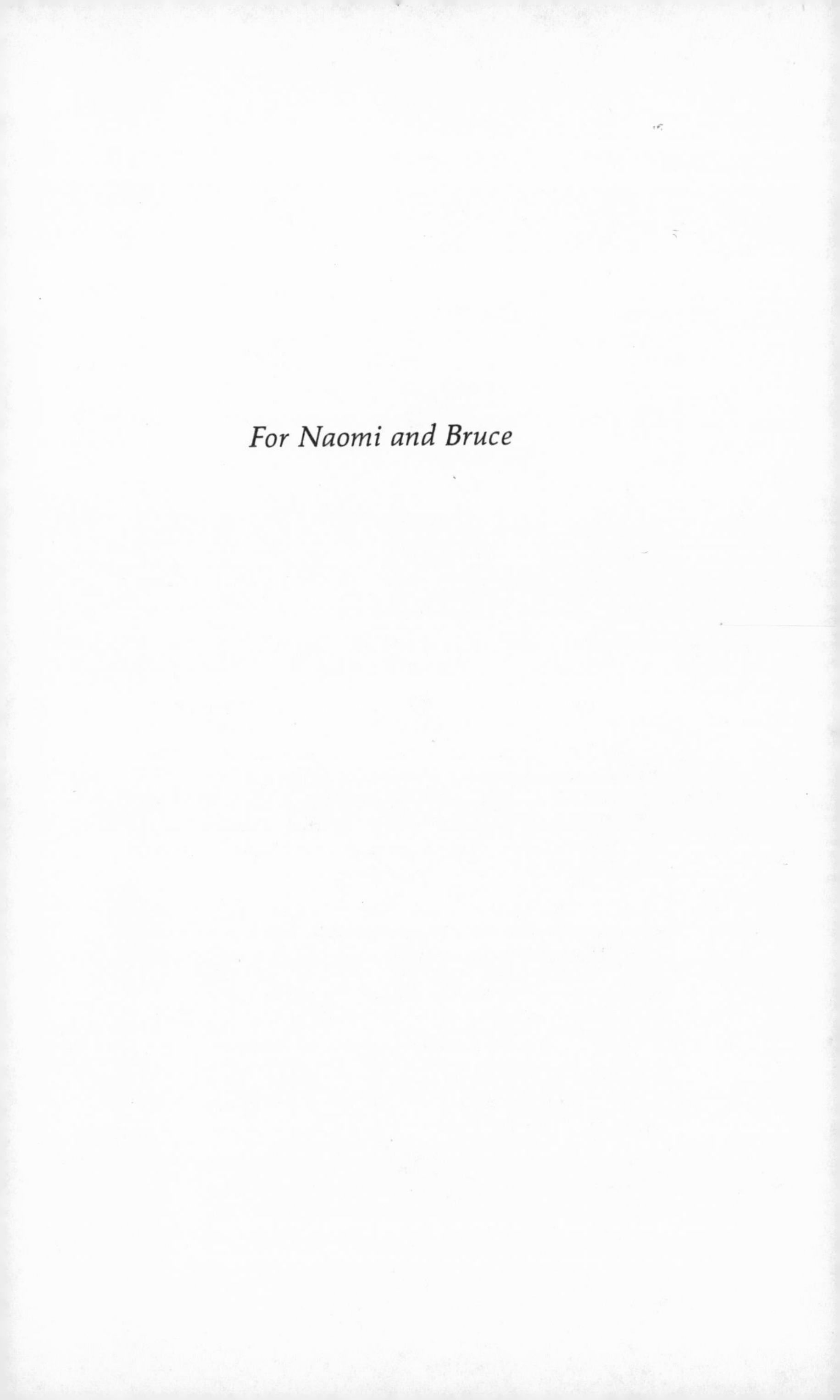

For Naomi and Bruce

Acknowledgments

Several of the chapters in this book are greatly expanded and rewritten versions of material that has appeared elsewhere. They are used here with the permission of the copyright owners, to whom my thanks.

The chapter on Franklin appeared in the book *Great Lives, Great Deeds* under the title "The Incomparable Ben Franklin." Copyright © 1964 The Reader's Digest Association, Inc.

The chapter on Jefferson appeared in *The Reader's Digest*, March 1963, under the title "Our Legacy from Mr. Jefferson." Copyright © 1963 The Reader's Digest Association, Inc.

The chapter on Emerson appeared in *The Reader's Digest*, August 1960, under the title "Emerson's Vital Message." Copyright © 1960 The Reader's Digest Association, Inc.

The chapter on Thoreau appeared in *The Reader's Digest*, December 1961, under the title "Mr. Thoreau of Walden Pond." Copyright © 1961 The Reader's Digest Association, Inc.

Permissions

Contents

Preface

THIS BOOK is a love letter to six great Americans. Some of them certainly had faults, and plenty of historians have written about them, but I have preferred to dwell chiefly on their virtues. Looking back on these individuals, who lived through periods of great difficulty and danger to the Republic, seems to me a valuable enterprise in a time when so many Americans are troubled about the present and fearful about the future of our nation.

Why these six, and not others? I have chosen them mainly because each seems to me to have embodied in his or her own person a special American characteristic of importance. Franklin was, among so many other things, the first self-made man, a pioneer in breaking the barriers of class. Adams embodied the Puritan characteristics including what is now called the work ethic. Jefferson, the first and greatest American democrat, was, like Franklin, a multisided genius, who revealed the versatility and flexibility which still continue to surprise many Europeans. Sojourner Truth spoke—and how magnificently!—for all the victims of injustice based on color or sex. Emerson was the American scholar who broke the bonds of parochial deference to the Old World. Thoreau, who created—or re-created—the counterculture, saw before anyone else the dangers of unlimited exploitation of the continent's resources and the folly of treating Nature as an enemy, rather than a friend.

What are the qualities and circumstances that have made for distinction in a select few in the America of the past two centuries? Some comment on this subject is to be found in the individual chapters of this book, and I have added a few more observations at the end.

These six are of course not the only great Americans whom I admire; I have a long list, beginning, like everyone's, with Lincoln and Washington. If my book were five times as long, and written in a different framework, I should have liked to say something about Justices Holmes and Brandeis, Booker T. Washington, Franklin and Eleanor Roosevelt, Susan B. Anthony, Helen Keller, Jane Addams, and so many more—explorers, inventors, writers, painters, architects, social reformers, political figures—not forgetting the nameless hundreds who risked their lives by running the Underground Railroad before the Civil War, or the Chinese workingmen who clung by their fingernails to the cliffs of the Sierra and built the hardest part of the first transcontinental railroad.

As I have done six times before, I wish to express

my deep thanks to Rose Emery Bliven for her very great help, and for moral support far above and beyond the call of marital duty.

Bruce Bliven
Stanford, California

A Mirror for Greatness:

Six Americans

one

Benjamin Franklin: The Bourgeois Genius

OF THE great heroes of the American past, most seem rather formidable. Washington was so austerely perfect that even those closest to him were a little afraid of him. Jefferson was always genial, but people were awed by his intellect. Lincoln had the common touch—none more so—yet his image is tinged with sadness.

But there is one famous person, the quintessential American, of whom no one can think without a mental half-smile. Benjamin Franklin, editor, printer, inventor, scientist, writer, and statesman, was a very great man, in some ways the greatest this continent has produced, but his image is so friendly, so homely, that our affection for him has no reservations. Though his achievements were tremendous, his character appeared simple, his personality charming, his sense of humor delicious. You feel that if he walked into your home tonight, in five minutes he would seem like a member of the family.

Franklin was so versatile that few appreciate how extraordinary he was. Only the historians fully appreciate his great achievements in the Revolution. Only the scientists recognize the breadth and depth of his curiosity and knowledge. Only the writers can savor the art behind his seemingly artless prose. On the two-hundred-and-fiftieth anniversary of his birth, *five hundred* scientific and other learned bodies throughout the world, led by the Franklin Institute of Philadelphia, joined in the celebration. His versatility had been so great that the meeting had to be divided into ten parts: (1) science, invention, and engineering; (2) statesmanship; (3) education and the study of nature; (4) finance, insurance, commerce, and industry; (5) mass communication; (6) printing, advertising, and the graphic arts; (7) religion, fraternal organizations, and the humanities; (8) medicine and public health; (9) agriculture; (10) music and recreation.

The seeming simplicity of his character was to some degree an illusion; he was a complicated man with multiple roles. When we study carefully his writings and those of his contemporaries who discussed him, we come to realize that he functioned on three levels. The first is the one recognized in his own time, and embracing the view of him that most people hold even today, the homespun philosopher, full of shrewdness and cunning—in short, Poor Richard of the *Almanac* that he published for many years. He believed in what he wrote in the *Almanac,* but Poor Richard was a fictional character, shallow in comparison with Franklin himself.

The second was Franklin the statesman, the devoted patriot who spent the last part of his long life in unflagging service to his country, the man without whom the Revolution might have failed. He was utterly sincere in what he did for America, but even this role did not plumb his greatest depths. The third and innermost Franklin was the scientist, filled with inexhaustible curiosity, one of the two greatest, with Sir Isaac Newton, of the era.

Franklin, born in 1706, was the eighth of ten children of his father's second wife; if modern ideas of small families had prevailed he would never have been born at all. His father was a poor tallow merchant and candlemaker; Ben was to become the first self-made American, breaking the rigid class bonds that existed in the colonies as they did in England.

He learned to read very early; at seven he was writing poems and sending them to his uncle in

London. At the age of ten, after less than one year of formal schooling, he was put to work by his father. Ben, who grew up to dine with kings and at his death was probably the most famous private citizen in the world, taught himself almost everything he knew, including science, philosophy, music, French, German, Spanish, Italian, Latin, and an intimate familiarity with the great classic authors.

At twelve, he was apprenticed to his brother, a Boston printer, himself only in his early twenties. That same year, Ben wrote two ballads which were printed and peddled successfully in the fashion of the day. One celebrated the capture of the notorious pirate Blackbeard; the other—a huge success—told of the drowning of a local lighthouse keeper's family.

At seventeen, he was writing anonymous contributions to his brother's newspaper, slipping them under the printing-office door at night; they were published and became tremendously popular. One of his contributions purported to be the confessions of an elderly widow who had had an exceptionally stormy life. Her story was so realistic and plausible that many subscribers took it for granted that she was genuine.

That same year, after friction with his brother, he left home and sought work, unsuccessfully, as a printer in New York. Hearing of a possible job in Philadelphia, he went there—journeying much of the way on foot. Some of the distance he traveled by a boat down the Delaware, and although he had paid his passage, he volunteered to take a hand at the oars, proving so useful that, when they arrived, the boatmen demurred at taking his money. Generations of American schoolchildren have heard how on arrival he spent almost his last coppers for three puffy rolls of bread, walked down the street eating one, with the other two under his arms—and was laughed at by the girl who afterward became his wife.

Franklin was desperately determined to improve himself. At only fourteen or fifteen, admiring *The Spectator,* which contains the famous essays of Addison and Steele, he copied them out to get the rhythm, then waited awhile and tried to reproduce them from memory. He paraphrased them in verse to improve his vocabulary. Sometimes, studying the logic of an argument, he listed the main points on cards, shuffled them, and after some time tried to sort them out properly.

He firmly believed that by conscious self-discipline you can improve your character. "It is an art to be studied," he said, "like painting or music." Looking back in his old age, he was convinced that he had been at least partially successful in this effort.

At seventeen, he wrote down four rules he should obey: (1) save money; (2) don't promise anybody more than you can perform; (3) don't try to "get rich quick;" (4) don't gossip; on the contrary, "Speak all the good I know of everybody."

When still a young man he made a list of thirteen admirable qualities to pursue. He would be temperate in eating and drinking, avoid idle chatter, be systematic in business, fulfill every task he undertook, avoid extravagance, eliminate idleness and wasted motion, be sincere, treat others fairly, bear unfairness patiently, be clean, not let trifles upset him, be chaste, and seek humility.

This tall order Franklin pursued systematically. He made "a little book, in which I allotted a page for each of the virtues . . . I determined to give a week's strict attention to each of them successively." Since there were thirteen items, he could get through them four times each year, writing down the degree of success he was obtaining. He followed this routine for a long time, and afterward believed that it had helped, though this was certainly not equally true of all thirteen of his points. He was, for example, so untidy that any room where he worked was soon heaped with books, documents, letters, and other impedimenta; with his brilliant memory he could instantly retrieve anything he wanted, though no one else could. A more serious dereliction, by Puritan standards, was the fact that all his life he was notoriously fond of feminine company.

Franklin was the greatest example in his century of the characteristically American philosophy which William James, a century later, called Pragmatism: Accept circumstances as you find them, face the facts without pretending they are otherwise, do the best you can, and don't fret because your best is not perfection.

The boy was a trained printer, and a good one, and soon after arriving in Philadelphia he had a job. A few months later, he was the victim of a cruel hoax by the

Colonial Governor of Pennsylvania, Sir William Keith. Having met Ben by accident, he took an instantaneous liking to him, as did nearly everyone else. Sir William, who had a pathological habit of making promises he could not fulfill, persuaded him to go to London to buy printing equipment, promising money and credentials which never arrived. Franklin, at eighteen, landed penniless—and never heard from the Governor. But his trade stood him in good stead; he got a job as a printer, and was speedily the top man in the shop. He was so strong that he could carry two heavy forms of metal type up a flight of stairs, whereas the other men could carry only one. In spite of the cruel mistreatment he had received from the Governor, he never complained about him. Ben's only comment was, "He wished to please everybody, and having little to give, he gave expectations."

When he had to set the type on a book of philosophy, he was moved to write a pamphlet of his own. He was nineteen years old. It was called *A Dissertation on Liberty and Necessity, Pleasure and Pain*. The pamphlet did not attract much attention, but it brought him some friends among British intellectuals who proved useful during his later long years in London.

A few months later, Ben was offered a position in a shop that was to be set up in Philadelphia, and was advanced enough money to pay for his return voyage. Before the shop could open, the man who planned it died, and Ben fell back on his trade as a printer. He was soon offered another job at good wages, one of his duties being to train apprentices who were paid much less; Franklin accidentally learned that his employer intended to wait until the apprentices were adept and then dismiss the teacher, saving his high wage.

Two years later, with a partner, Ben set up a printing office of his own, and two years later still—he was even now only twenty-four—he borrowed money and bought out the partner.

He was an indefatigable worker; often he slaved all night, if it was necessary, to deliver printed matter on time. When he bought a new stock of paper, he himself trundled it through the streets of Philadelphia in a wheelbarrow, thus at one stroke giving the impression of being a modest, hardworking fellow, and that his business was doing well.

His printing office served other purposes. He sold stationery, as might have been expected, and also books, which gave him the chance to read them himself before someone bought them.

Not only did he sell books, but he published them, including a volume on home doctoring for people and one for animals, books of poetry, and religious tracts. He issued Samuel Richardson's *Pamela*, the first novel ever to appear in America. In addition to his almanacs and newspapers he was the official printer for Pennsylvania and printed all official state documents. He also offered for sale salves and ointments.

In 1730, Franklin married. At about the same time, he became the father of an illegitimate son; the mother is not known. Ben and his wife brought up the boy, William, in their household, with their own daughter; he grew up to be a Tory and the British Governor of New Jersey.

In 1732, at twenty-six, Franklin started his famous *Poor Richard's Almanac,* which instantly became a huge success. An almanac was at that time almost the only printed matter in addition to the Bible that was found in every American home. It gave all needed information about the sun, moon, and tides, predicted the weather a year in advance, gave medical information, and filled up the odd spaces with maxims and bits of philosophy. He made "Poor Richard" Saunders, the supposed author, so real that he overshadowed Ben himself—and in the minds of many people, still does.

At one time, Poor Richard complained bitterly in the *Almanac* about people who questioned whether he really existed, at that time a subject of lively debate. "This is not civil treatment, to endeavor to deprive me of my very being." To those who thought he must be getting rich he denied it, saying that the printer (who was Ben himself!) took most of the money. He even attacked Franklin by name, for being stupid:

> Ben beats his pate and fancies wit will come;
> But he may knock; there's nobody at home.

One year, "Mrs. Poor Richard" claimed to have scratched out Richard's preface and written her own. He was giving her too much publicity, she said: "Cannot I have a little fault or two but all the country must see it in print?" While her husband was away she had gone through the *Almanac* and made all the weather better—for the sake of housewives hanging out their clothes.

Dozens of the maxims in the *Almanac* are still in use, though few realize their origin. Franklin never pretended he had invented all of them, but even those he borrowed he often sharpened by rewriting. When an old Scottish proverb said, "A gloved cat was never a good hunter," Franklin said, "The cat in gloves catches no mice." Everyone knows: "Early to bed and early to rise, makes a man healthy, wealthy, and wise"; "Experience keeps a dear school, yet fools will learn in no other"; "He that goes a-borrowing goes a-sorrowing"; "Nothing is inevitable but death and taxes"; "Fish and visitors smell in three days"; "Half a truth is often a great lie."

Others that are less familiar are equally full of the distilled wisdom of the ages: "Now I have a sheep and a cow, everybody bids me good morrow"; "He does not possess wealth; wealth possesses him"; "Approve not of him who commends all you say"; "The absent are never without fault, nor the present without excuse"; "Let thy maidservant be faithful, strong—and homely"; "Sin is not hurtful because it is forbidden, but it is forbidden because it is hurtful"; "He is not well bred that cannot bear ill breeding in others"; "Having been poor is no shame, but being ashamed of it is"; "The brave and the wise can both pity and excuse, when cowards and fools show no mercy"; "Love your neighbor—yet don't pull down your hedge"; "It is ill manners to silence a fool and cruelty to let him go on."

He professed to welcome the idea that he occasionally made an enemy, since this helped his own character. Once he observed of such a man, "Since 'tis convenient to have at least one enemy who, by his readiness to revile one on all occasions may make one careful of one's conduct. I shall keep him an enemy for that purpose."

His lifelong rule was never to answer his hostile critics. "Censures I have generally passed over in silence, conceiving when they were just that I ought rather to amend than defend; and when they were undeserved, that a little time would justify me." Similarly, he observed, "I leave [my philosophical opinions] to take their chance in the world. If they are right, truth and experience will support them; if wrong, they ought to be refuted and rejected."

When his work on electricity was published in France, a theologian there attacked him furiously, but Franklin declined to answer. "I concluded to let my papers shift for themselves, believing it was better to spend what time I could spare from public business in making new experiments than in disputing those already made." A friend who was a scientist reduced the critic to mincemeat, and he is remembered today only in footnotes to biographies of Franklin.

Ben was lied about cruelly by the few people who did not like him. While he was in London getting the Stamp Act repealed, word was spread in the colonies that he was himself the author of the outrageous impost. As usual, he did not bother to answer. "When truth and error have fair play, the former is always an overmatch for the latter."

As an editor he insisted on airing both sides of controversies, though many thought all opinions contrary to their own should be suppressed. Said Ben, "If all [editors] were determined not to print anything till they were sure it would offend nobody, there would be very little printed."

In 1732 appeared the first issue of *Poor Richard's Almanac*; it continued until 1758, though for the last few years he left most of the details to others. In the year that the *Almanac* ended, he gathered an anthology of the maxims and bits of philosophy from all the previous issues and published them as a book, *The Way to Wealth*. It had a large sale, by the standards of the day, not only in the colonies and in England but on the Continent.

At the height of his success, Ben was the best-known writer of the English-speaking world. His *Almanac* sold ten thousand copies a year, a huge circulation in the sparsely populated colonies. His *Autobiography*, though he never found time to finish it, is one of the most widely read in the world. He began it in 1771, in London, and wrote the first half of it in only two weeks, from memory, recording correctly names and dates of forty or fifty years earlier. His newspapers and his magazine were successful in direct proportion to the percentage of the content that came from his own pen.

The quarter century of his life beginning with his

return from the disastrous trip to London was probably the happiest and most fruitful in Franklin's life. His creative imagination gave birth to a variety of projects, including the first professional police force, the first volunteer fire company, the first fire-insurance company, the school that became the University of Pennsylvania, and the world-famous Pennsylvania Hospital.

In 1727, he established the famous club, the Junto, or Leather Apron Club, which met regularly for its members to exchange ideas and information, the forerunner of all the service clubs of today. There were twelve members, and Franklin drew up a list of twenty-four stock questions to be asked at each meeting. They amounted to saying: What's going on in town? Have any interesting strangers arrived lately? Do any of the members need help of any kind? (Franklin himself was occasionally assisted during his lean years with modest loans from the Junto.) Each member in turn had to write an essay and read it aloud at a meeting, or prepare himself to lead a discussion on a philosophical subject. The Junto continued for thirty years.

The following year, 1728, he set up business with a partner as a printer, as I have recorded. In 1729 the partners bought a newspaper, *The Pennsylvania Gazette;* Franklin's contributions—he wrote nearly all the news—and his furious energy in attending to the details soon turned it into a highly profitable enterprise. In 1730, as noted, he borrowed money and bought out his partner. In 1731, he established the

Library Company, one of the first subscription libraries in America. Busy as he was, he spent an hour or two in the library each day, and thereby gave himself the equivalent of a thorough college education.

As always, Franklin poured out advice on every possible subject. When the people of Philadelphia began digging up the landscape in search of mythical pirate treasure, Franklin told them of the farmer who gave a piece of land to his son, remarking: "I assure Thee I have found a considerable quantity of gold by digging there; Thou mayst do the same. But Thee must carefully observe this: *Never dig more than plow-deep.*"

As a young man he participated in an expedition against Indians in western Pennsylvania, and one day the chaplain complained to him that the soldiers were negligent in attending the daily prayer meetings. In those times each soldier was served a daily portion of rum, and Ben advised the man of the cloth to become also the rum steward. "If you were to deal it out, and only just after prayers, you would have them all about you." The chaplain followed his recommendation and Franklin afterward noted, "Never were prayers more generally and more punctually attended."

On this expedition, many horses and wagons were needed, and the farmers came forward with them only reluctantly. Franklin personally guaranteed that they would be returned or paid for—risking the loss of a huge sum that he did not have. At the same time he delicately hinted that if the horses and wagons were not supplied voluntarily they would be commandeered. The combination of the carrot and the stick seemed to work.

When his wife's prayer book was stolen from her church pew, Franklin published a note in his newspaper: "The person who took it is desired to open it and read the Eighth Commandment, and afterward return it into the same pew again; upon which no further notice will be taken."

His appearance commanded instant liking and respect. His glance was steady and kindly; he had big gray eyes set in a large face, a wide and humorous mouth, and as a young man, ample blond hair. His were the deft hands of a printer. As a rule he spoke little and slowly, though he was quick to act. He had a remarkable ability to attract friends. At one time he got the contract to print the paper money for the colony of New Jersey and went to Burlington for this purpose; the members of the New Jersey Council met him at that time and became his friends for life.

A host of stories illustrate his remarkable character. He made it a lifelong rule to continue to trust his friends until they proved untrustworthy; as a young man, this sometimes got him into trouble, but he never regretted it. "One should make it a rule," he wrote, "always to suppose one's friends may be right till one finds them wrong, rather than to suppose them wrong till one finds them right." When he was still in his teens, a young man of his own age borrowed money from him that he was holding in trust for someone else, and then ran away. It took Ben years to pay back the owner, but he complained of the theft only mildly. A second friend borrowed money and then provoked a quarrel in order to justify repudiating the debt; Franklin said long afterward, "I loved him notwithstanding, for he had many amiable qualities." In Philadelphia an alcoholic partner nearly ruined their business, but Franklin would take no steps to break the relationship until the other man suggested it.

He was by all odds the most distinguished newspaper editor of his day in the English-speaking world. He once remarked that any good newspaper editor should know languages, write clearly and simply, and have a knowledge of military strategy, biography, history, the national policies of various countries, and the manners and customs of all nations. He added, "Men thus accomplished are very rare in this remote part of the world." This was a great understatement since there was only one: Ben himself.

Franklin knew how many there are who will try to get around you by flattery—and what insidious incense to the nostrils this can be. He liked to tell the story of two farmhands who had been sent to fetch a heavy piece of machinery, one of them a lazy fellow and the other vain of his strength. When they arrived where the machinery was, the lazy man promptly said the piece was so heavy that two of them could not possibly carry it. The other, as his sly companion had anticipated, insisted that he could do so alone—and carried it the whole way.

Criticized by readers of his newspaper, Franklin answered in print that it is hopeless to take advice from everybody and told what he called "an old fable" of a man and his son who were taking a donkey to town. (In fact, it was taken from Aesop, somewhat changed.) Since the way was bad, the old man rode, and was promptly scolded by the first passerby for letting his boy wade through the mud. Accordingly, the boy also mounted, whereupon the next traveler reproached them for overloading the beast. The old man dismounted, only to have his son abused in a fresh encounter for riding while his father was on foot. With both dismounted, they were next called fools for tramping in the mud when they could be riding. Thereupon the father, exclaiming that it was impossible to please everybody, threw the donkey over the next bridge they came to.

He told his fellow writers not to worry if people disagreed with or ignored them. If you can reach even a small minority with the truth, you may have an important influence—as he himself did with some thoughtful Britons before the Revolution. Though your writings "may be lightly passed over by many readers, yet if they make a deep impression on one active mind in a hundred the effect may be considerable."

As a boy, Ben liked to argue belligerently, but he soon realized peo[illegible]re rarely persuaded by a frontal attack, and forced h[illegible]e a different technique. He learned the Socratic method of asking questions which, if given an honest reply, will force your opponent to change his mind. "Quarreling," he remarked, "is like an insect bite which can infect you if you scratch it." In his old age he was able to say, "For these fifty years past, no one has ever heard a dogmatic expression escape me."

In 1736, he was chosen clerk of the Pennsylvania Legislature, and held that post until he was elected a member a few years later. In 1737, he became Philadelphia Postmaster, and devised an ingenious method of persuading people in the town to come to the post office to pick up their mail. In each issue of *The Pennsylvania Gazette* he printed the names of those who had mail waiting for them; if they came in promptly, they received it with no additional charge beyond what the correspondent had paid; if they were dilatory, it was delivered to the home at a cost of a penny—a much larger amount than the same sum would be today.

In 1740, he invented the famous Franklin stove, still in use in country areas, using about half the fuel required by earlier ones. The Franklin stove has a grate, sliding doors, and a flue which doubles back and forms something like a hot-air radiator. He refused to patent it, saying, "As we enjoy great advantages from the inventions of others, we should be glad of an opportunity to serve others by any invention of ours."

In 1745, the indefatigable Ben laid plans for the American Philosophical Society, an important enterprise that continues to the present day. For half a century it was a national academy of science, the first national library and museum, and the first patent office. The federal government consulted it constantly on every sort of scientific question. Among its later presidents was Jefferson, and among the members have been Washington, Hamilton, John Adams, Lafayette, Tom Paine, Baron von Steuben, Audubon, Fulton, Emerson, Whittier, and Oliver Wendell Holmes, Sr. Members abroad have included Darwin, Pasteur, and Madame Curie. Ninety-four of its members have won Nobel Prizes.

Ben's influence was so strong that, thirty years after his death, the Franklin Institute was created to honor his memory. It still flourishes, specializing in something dear to Franklin's heart, interpreting science and technology for the layman. Its annual medals to outstanding scientists are highly valued; among the recipients have been Thomas Edison, Guglielmo Marconi, Orville Wright, Albert Einstein, and Enrico Fermi.

In 1747 Franklin proved his courage, as he had done many times before and was to do many times again. There were French and Spanish pirates off Delaware Bay, and they were threatening to come up the river and loot Philadelphia; they actually did come as far as Newcastle, where they captured a ship and murdered the captain.

The Pennsylvania Legislature was dominated by the Quakers who refused to vote money for defense. Franklin, following his usual habit, wrote and circulated a pamphlet about the danger and then proceeded to raise a militia of ten thousand volunteers, who armed themselves, drilled, and succeeded in frightening the pirates away. When money was needed for a fort and a cannon, the pragmatic Franklin organized a lottery and raised the money. The militia insisted that the reluctant Ben be their commander. After the first public review, they paraded home with him, a special honor, and fired a final salute before his house; the reverberations broke some of his delicate electrical equipment.

In the following year, at the age of forty-two, Franklin retired from active participation in his many business activities, which included investments in several enterprises, some of them in colonies distant from Pennsylvania. He had an income from the printing business and other profitable ventures that may have been the equivalent of $30,000 today. He proposed to devote most of his time for the rest of his life to science and to public service, and he did.

Of great importance, in the perspective of history, was his career in science. Franklin was the father of the modern use of electricity, on which our whole civilization is so largely built today. For thousands of years, men had known that certain substances, when rubbed together, developed singular properties of attraction or repulsion. Early in the eighteenth century, men found that this unusual effect was especially strong when glass was rubbed with a fabric such as silk. Under special conditions, this rubbing could also produce sparks. By the time Franklin became interested, the art had advanced to a crude device for producing electricity, and a means of storage, a Leyden jar. Within a short time, he had learned more about electricity than all previous experimenters combined. He was struck by the ability of a pointed metal rod to collect static electricity, and it is almost certain that, with a great forward leap of the intellect, he reasoned that the charge of a thundercloud, manifested in lightning, existed there in static form and might be drawn down into a pointed iron rod. From this it followed that such an iron rod, attached to a building, might bring down the static charge, or even deflect the lightning itself if it were about to strike very close by. If this is how he reasoned, he had invented the lightning rod. The idea of grounding the rod in the earth was quickly added.

I say "almost certain," because, oddly enough, he never wrote a word about the one thing everybody knows about him. This is his experiment, during a thunderstorm, of flying a kite made out of a silk handkerchief, with a piece of wire extending from it, bringing static electricity down the cord, and producing sparks by placing his knuckle close to a metal key tied to the lower end. This world-famous experiment presumably took place in June 1752; but it was never mentioned until fifteen years later. Then it was reported in a book on electricity by Joseph Priestley which Ben encouraged him to write and of which he read the manuscript. The report is so detailed that it seems obvious he must have told Priestley the story, though we can only guess that this is true. He did, however, shortly after similar experiments had been made in France, describe these in his newspaper, and also print instructions for constructing a lightning rod.

It is hard for people to realize today what a godsend the lightning rod was. Buildings then were constructed of brick or stone, or—overwhelmingly, in America—of wood, and a direct hit by lightning could do great harm to the structure and the people within. A lightning rod, carefully placed, could minimize this danger. In September 1752, a month before he printed his account of the lightning rod, Ben put one on his own house, and a few years later, while he was away in London, it saved the home from being damaged.

Neither Franklin nor anyone else realized the power of the natural force with which they were experimenting. Franklin once tried to kill a turkey with an electric shock and was knocked unconscious; a Swedish physicist, experimenting in Russia, put up a rod, did not ground it, and got killed.

All Europe soon proclaimed Franklin for his magnificent achievements in electricity. Immanuel Kant said he "was a new Prometheus who had stolen fire from heaven." Carl Van Doren says that "with what seemed the simplest key he had unlocked one of the darkest and most terrifying doors in the unknown universe. Here was another hero of the human race, even as against the terrifying gods."

To this day, many people do not realize the extent of his scientific knowledge in this field. He insisted that electricity was a single "fluid," not two, as had been believed. He first used the terms *positive* and *negative,* and by using glass and lead plates in series, he had invented the electrical condenser, employed today in every radio, television set, telephone circuit, and many other types of apparatus. He foreshadowed the electron theory and the electric battery. Among the things he discovered and named are the battery, conductor, charge and discharge. It is believed that he improved the electrostatic machine that generates electricity by friction.

Honors soon came thick and fast. In 1755 this man from Boston, who had had only about one year's instruction at a dame's school, got honorary degrees from Harvard and Yale and a gold medal from the Royal Society in London. He was to get other honorary degrees, from William and Mary College in Virginia, from St. Andrews in Scotland, and from Oxford. Finally, he was elected a member of the Royal Society, a tremendous honor for a colonial. His book on the subject was translated into German and Italian, and sold widely; eventually he was an honorary member of twenty learned societies all over Europe. In 1753, when he had received some of these honors but this fact was not widely known, he told a friend he was like the girl described in a magazine, "who was observed to grow suddenly proud, and none could guess the reason, till it came to be known that she had got on a new pair of garters."

Though his greatest achievements dealt with electricity, Franklin had far broader interests. He studied heat, light, sound, magnetism, chemistry, geology, physiology, psychology, and oceanography. He discovered rotary storms; he heard of a northeast storm in Boston very similar to the northeast storm in Philadelphia a few hours earlier. Getting newspapers of the same date from all the colonies, he checked the times at which each storm had occurred and found that they had traveled from southwest to northeast, though each one struck from the northeast, deducing that the storm consisted of a rotary air mass. Crossing the ocean and observing waterspouts, he was the first to realize that a column of warm air is forced upward, carrying water with it, by the cool, heavier air from the surrounding region. He also discovered that water does not invariably boil at 212 degrees Fahrenheit, but that the thinner the atmosphere, the lower the boiling point.

He was the father of aerodynamics; sailors told him it is hard to row a boat in shallow water. He figured out that displacement of water by the boat is the reason, built a model, and proved it. He was also the father of jet propulsion, suggesting that a boat would move forward if a stream of water were ejected from the stern at high speed.

The most amazing of all his forward leaps of the imagination in the field of science came in 1782. He actually surmised that the interior of the earth might be a molten fluid, and that the continents might be a shell, floating in some conflict on the surface. Only in the 1970s did earth scientists come to much the same conclusion.

He came close to the germ theory when he noted that people do not catch cold from exposure but when several of them are closed up in a room without ventilation. He sat naked in his bedroom every morning busily reading or writing, which must have been quite a spectacle. He believed that by thus adapting his skin to varying temperatures he was better able to resist infection. In an era when most people ate and drank hugely, and very few took exercise, he preached and practiced moderation in eating and drinking, and sang the praises of walking. He noted sensibly that of every hundred fevers, ninety-two cured themselves, four were fatal, and the doctors perhaps ameliorated the last few. When he visited St. Andrews to receive an honorary degree, a student there, Lord Cardross, was gravely ill of a fever, and the doctor wanted him blistered, the fashionable remedy of the moment. Franklin argued strongly against it, and with his great prestige, prevented it and possibly saved the young man's life.

He discovered the Gulf Stream and urged ship captains to take advantage of it. By putting squares of light- and dark-colored cloth down on a snowbank he learned that light colors reflect heat; Europeans living in the tropics needed about a hundred years to take his advice and dress in white. In his old age he invented bifocal spectacles, that blessing of the elderly.

Franklin was the father of daylight saving. When he arrived in Paris he was shocked to see how many of the inhabitants slept until almost midday. In a comical essay that he prudently did not publish immediately, he assured the Parisians that the sun rises every day at dawn, and not at noon, as they seemed to think, and the idea of daylight saving followed as a logical consequence.

Annoyed by the numerous sounds that are given to many letters, he invented a new alphabet in which each letter had only one sound—that was reinvented in the 1960s and proved a useful device in teaching children to read. He discovered that ants can communicate; when he suspended a jar of sweet syrup from the ceiling by a string, first one ant found it and then an army came, showing that the first had reported his bonanza. When people became ill after drinking Jamaica rum, it was Franklin who investigated and reported that the cause was lead poisoning, resulting from the use of lead pipes in the distilling process. He invented the use of chemical fertilizer; he put gypsum on a field, making the grass much greener, and arranged it so that the stripes of greener grass spelled out words!

Franklin devised a number of gadgets, some of which are employed to this day. One of these was a table whose height could be adjusted; another was a mechanical "hand" at the end of a pole, to pick books off a high shelf—used even now in many stores. His kitchen ladder that folds down into a stool is still popular.

He was a skillful musician, who sang, played the harp, guitar, and violin, and wrote learnedly of problems connected with composing music. He improved a rudimentary musical instrument called the glass harmonica; in his version special glasses of different sizes were manufactured, fastened to a rod, and rotated by a handle while partly submerged in water. When touched by the hand while rotating they gave off a sweet sound; Franklin used thirty-seven glasses, which gave him three octaves, including sharps and flats. His invention spread rapidly through England and several European countries and enjoyed a great vogue for forty years. Beethoven, Mozart, Gluck, and others composed music especially for this instrument.

Public affairs soon pressed in on the scientist, engaging nearly all his time and energy. In 1753 he was made Deputy Postmaster General for the Northern Colonies and greatly improved the postal service in this area. He speeded up the mail between New York and Philadelphia from once a week to three times a week, in summer, and from once a fortnight to once a week in winter. Mail went to England with unheard-of frequency, once a month. Post roads, the only through roads there were, extended all the way from Canada to Florida.

For eighteen years, from 1757 to 1775, except for a return home between 1762 and 1764, Franklin was in London. He went originally to lobby in Parliament to force the heirs of William Penn to pay local taxes on their enormous land holdings in Pennsylvania, but he soon became the official London representative for that colony. Later he added Georgia, New Jersey, and Massachusetts.

While his return to America during this period lasted only about two years, he performed tremendously important services during this time. The Indians had risen again on the distant frontier, and there was great bitterness against them among the white riffraff in eastern Pennsylvania. These individuals had no intention of going to fight the Indians who were actually misbehaving; on the contrary, they rose against the innocent Red Men living near by, who had dwelt in peace and friendship with their white neighbors for a hundred years. Many were murdered, with the utmost savagery. Franklin, in what was by now almost a reflex action on his part, wrote a pamphlet in protest, and in it he made a classic statement of the case against racism:

> If an Indian injures me, does it follow that I may revenge that injury on all Indians? It is well known that Indians are of different tribes, nations, and languages, as well as the white people. In Europe, if the French, who are white people, should injure the Dutch, are they to revenge it on the English, because they too are white people? The only crime of these poor wretches seems to have been that they had a reddish-brown skin and black hair; and some people of that sort, it seems, had murdered some of our relations. If it be right to kill men for such a reason, then, should any man with a freckled face and red hair kill a wife or child of mine, it would be right for me to revenge it by killing all the freckled, red-haired men, women, and children I could afterward anywhere meet with.

The riotous mobs planned to attack some peaceable Indians who had taken refuge in Philadelphia, and the frightened Governor of Pennsylvania appealed to Franklin for help. Franklin, with great courage, faced the mob and shamed them out of their plan. But he took his own part in the episode lightly. Writing to a friend in London, he commented:

> Within four and twenty hours, your old friend was a common soldier, a councillor, a kind of dictator, an ambassador to a country mob, and, on his returning home, nobody again.

The Penn heirs, the rulers of Pennsylvania, had

become bitter enemies of Franklin, and especially since he had gone to London to try to force them to pay taxes. Relations rapidly worsened during his visit home, with a flurry of angry pamphlets from both sides. The heirs spread lying propaganda against him, but seemingly without much effect. The elected Assembly (Legislature) was on Franklin's side. Finally, the only course open for the patriots seemed to be a petition by the Assembly to the King in London, and Franklin sailed back to present it.

His usefulness to his country during the next eleven years was even greater than it had been before. He was a brilliant propagandist, perhaps the most successful in American history. He lectured, wrote pamphlets, and with his irresistible personal charm made many friends for himself and for his country; some of them formed the pro-American block in Parliament which was of tremendous value, especially in the period after the Revolution. With great skill, he persuaded Parliament to abolish the Stamp Tax, which had added heavy cost to many legal documents in the colonies. By doing so, he perhaps postponed the Revolution for a decade, giving the Americans badly needed time to prepare.

His brilliance as a writer made his propaganda pamphlets tremendously effective. In one case he published a mock *Edict by the King of Prussia,* laying claim to the whole of Great Britain with exactly the same false arguments by which the British King claimed the American colonies as his property. He caused a sensation.

Another powerful piece of propaganda that quickly

ran around the world was his *Rules by Which a Great Empire May be Reduced to a Small One.* The rules were a list of the unjust actions taken by England against America.

Sometimes his delicious sense of humor was more effective than any philippic could have been. Before the Revolution, a bitter grievance of the Americans was that the British dumped upon them thousands of convicted criminals who, on arriving, were turned loose to continue misbehaving. Franklin suggested, deadpan, that thousands of rattlesnakes be collected annually and sent to Britain to be turned loose in parks and gardens. Chasing them would give the British a world of healthy exercise. And they would still have an advantage over the Americans: "The rattlesnake gives warning before he attempts his mischief, which the convict does not."

Some of the English argued that it was proper to impose heavy burdens on American industry, because it was so rich, and Franklin solemnly recorded his agreement. "The very tails of the American sheep are so laden with wool that each has a little car or wagon on four little wheels to support and keep it from trailing on the ground."

An overexcited Englishman denounced the colonials for planning bootleg whale and cod fisheries on the Great Lakes, forgetting for the moment that these are freshwater, and Franklin conceded that this situation was serious. "Cod, when attacked by their enemies, fly into any water where they can be safest. Whales pursue them wherever they fly. The grand leap of a whale up Niagara Falls is esteemed one of the finest spectacles in nature."

In a more serious vein he answered English travelers returned from America who said that the colonists must be rich, they entertained so extravagantly. Said Franklin with iron common sense, a tourist is no judge; the Americans were just showing off before strangers.

One of the most terrible days of his life came during this period in London. He was accused of having illegally obtained, and circulated to a few people, private letters revealing that two Bostonians, who were supposed to be loyal Americans, were in fact secret English agents. Franklin was, of course, a British subject, and the Crown could have inflicted on him any punishment it chose. Hour after hour, he stood before a committee of the Privy Council, the executive organization under the King, while foul epithets were hurled at him, some so shocking that they were omitted from the printed record of the proceedings. A lesser man would have broken under the strain and gone to prison; Franklin stood like a rock, his face an expressionless mask. He cared nothing for his own dignity, everything for the welfare of America. He was punished only by being dismissed as Colonial Deputy Postmaster General.

Franklin survived the storm and continued to serve his country in London. He gave the British some valuable advice, part of which they took, and part they did not. In 1760, the British army had captured Canada from France; in the subsequent peace settlement, the English negotiators hesitated as to whether they should keep the great unexplored northern wilderness or the rich, sugar-producing island of Guadeloupe in the West Indies. Many people favored the latter, but Franklin persuaded the government that Canada would ultimately prove to be the greater prize.

Franklin did not return home until 1775, when it was generally apparent that full-scale war would come in the near future. As soon as he was back in America he was made a Pennsylvania delegate to the Second Continental Congress. Though at seventy he was twice the age of most of his fellow congressmen, he was appointed to serve on several committees, though not, as a rule, drafting their documents. His plain and simple style of writing, which seems so admirable to us today, was held to be unsuitable for public documents in a day of beflowered oratory.

He was elected a member of the Pennsylvania Legislature, and of the committee to write a new constitution for the colony, since the old British one would no longer do. Hard pressed with his work for the Continental Congress, he did not have much time for Pennsylvania. He did, however, make some important proposals that were adopted. He suggested an executive council instead of a governor; he had had enough of Pennsylvania governors. Every adult male taxpayer and his adult sons could vote; nobody could be a member of the State Legislature more than four years in every seven. Membership in the Legislature was to be based on the population of the various areas; the United States didn't get around to putting this sensible principle into practice until a Supreme Court decision in 1964.

At about this time, he wrote his famous letter to his old friend Andrew Strahan in England; Strahan was a member of Parliament and as such participated in the anti-American votes. Franklin began his letter, not with the nickname of "Straney" which he had often used, but formally with "Mr. Strahan," and went on:

> You are a member of Parliament, and one of that majority which has doomed my country to destruction. You have begun to burn our towns and murder our people. Look upon your hands! They are stained with the blood of your relations. You and I were long friends. You are now my enemy and I am Yours,
>
> B. Franklin.

Even in this bitter letter, he could not resist the whimsical wording at the end. Quite possibly he realized that the turn of this phrase would help to get his letter wide attention, as indeed it did.

On June 11, 1776, the Second Continental Congress appointed a committee to write a Declaration of Independence. It consisted of Adams, Franklin, Jefferson, Robert Livingston, and Roger Sherman, Jefferson being selected to do the drafting. Some members of the Congress made a few small changes in the first version, and Franklin, sitting beside the Virginian, noticed that he squirmed a little when the alterations were being made. To break the tension, Franklin told him a story about editing by committee. He knew a merchant, he said, who planned to put up a sign, "John Thompson, hatter, makes and sells hats for ready money," with a picture of a hat. One friend said the word "hatter" was superfluous, and others in turn said the same thing about "makes," "for ready money," and "sells." Someone then noted that with the picture, "hat" was not needed. The final signboard had only the drawing and the words "John Thompson."

Franklin himself seems to have made a few changes in the Declaration; at least they appear to be in his handwriting. When Jefferson wrote, "We hold these truths to be sacred and undeniable," Franklin changed it to "self evident." When the draft said, "But when a long train of abuses and usurpations, pursuing invariably the same object, evinces a design to reduce them to arbitrary power, it is their right . . . ," Franklin made it, "reduce them under absolute despotism. . . ."

At the signing, Franklin, who many years earlier had printed in his paper a drawing of a snake cut into sections, with the caption, "Join or die," is supposed to have made a remark with a similar meaning. John Hancock, after putting his dashing signature on the document, is supposed to have said, "We must be unanimous; there must be no pulling different ways; we must all hang together." Franklin was reported to have answered, "Yes, we must indeed all hang together or most assuredly we shall all hang separately." Since there is no contemporary record that he ever said this, we can only comment that it would have been like him.

Franklin was not to be long at home. It was of the utmost importance that America should achieve an alliance with France, England's almost perpetual enemy, without whose help the chance of winning independence would be very slim. Early in 1776, the Congress had sent Silas Deane to Paris as its representative and he had done well. But the matter was so important that Congress dispatched two men to aid him, Franklin and Arthur Lee, who was already in London.

Lee was a bad choice; he was a neurotic so extreme that he seemed almost insane; before long he was writing letters to the Congress accusing Deane of being a traitor, and was lying about Franklin in almost equally serious terms. For some reason, the Congress chose to accept Lee's word, and Deane was summoned home in disgrace, his career in ruins. (It took about sixty-five years for the government to admit it had made a mistake; it then publicly "rehabilitated" the long-dead Deane, and gave his heirs $37,000 as compensation.)

There were other troubles. The British blockade was so effective that much official mail never reached its destination, including the salaries of the Americans in Paris. The headquarters was a nest of spies; the paranoiac Lee, suspected all their employees—except his own secretary, who was in fact a British agent. Many letters were opened and read; sometimes they were sealed again and sent on, sometimes not. A "friend" of Franklin, who was a spy, took his letters out of their envelopes and substituted blank sheets of paper of the same size. Much information of importance was forwarded by these agents to the English government. The spies used their knowledge to gamble on the British stock exchange, and quarreled among themselves if one of them was suspected of withholding information from the others.

Franklin refused to get excited about the spies. He knew that chasing enemy agents is a full-time job, so he ignored them, remarking that he would be "concerned in no affairs that I should blush to have made public, and do nothing but what spies may see, and welcome." Ben knew that in fact the work of spies can be damaging in the extreme, but it was gamesmanship of a high order not to admit it.

In the darkest hours of the Revolution, when so many feared the cause was lost, Franklin's indomitable optimism was a tower of strength. He liked to recall the stranger who visited him when he was twenty-two and had just opened his own printing office. The man predicted that the enterprise would soon fail; Philadelphia was fast going downhill and the people were approaching bankruptcy. "Had I known him before I engaged in this business," Franklin commented long afterward, "probably I never should have done it."

This same man refused to buy a house, "because all was going to destruction." Later Ben reported, "At last I had the pleasure of seeing him give five times as much for one as he might have bought it for when he first began his croaking."

Franklin, after nearly eighteen years in London, was by now one of the most sophisticated men in the world, a student of languages, a foremost scientist; but the French for some reason decided that he was a simple wild man from the frontier, a born, homespun philosopher, perhaps Rousseau's natural savage, uncorrupted by the sickness of courts and great cities. Discovering how the wind blew, Franklin promptly began playing the role assigned to him; he cared nothing for his personal dignity if only he could serve his country well. On the cold November voyage he had worn a fur cap for warmth; it delighted the Parisians so much that he went on wearing it. To use spectacles in public was dreadfully unfashionable; he wore his and made them the fashion. When he was presented at Court he wore his old coat—he had no other. He wore no gold lace; he couldn't afford any. He had no wig—the one he had rented failed to arrive in time. The French, accustomed to nobility powdered, wigged, and arrayed in all the colors of the rainbow, were enchanted; they attached a mystic symbolism to his modest appearance. Franklin's public figure was not hurt by his gallantry toward the ladies, and in no time he was surrounded by a fluttering coterie of them.

In hardly more than a few weeks, he became the idol of Paris. His portrait was to be seen everywhere you looked; the city was filled with paintings, busts, miniatures, medallions, and prints of this delightful, simple American. The city's merchants commissioned artists to put his pictures on snuffboxes, rings, watches, clocks, vases, dishes, pocket knives, and even handkerchiefs.

When John Adams later came to Paris as a member of the American Commission, the puritanical Bostonian was shocked by what he considered Franklin's laziness; Adams was always up early and furiously at work at his desk; he could not understand the subtle diplomatic game Franklin was playing when he ignored his correspondence for days on end, and spent many hours at dinner with influential friends who could both tell him what was happening at Court and transmit his own shrewd suggestions to places where they might be very useful indeed.

His skillful diplomacy soon began to bear fruit, despite the blundering and even sabotage by Lee. The French wanted to help America, the enemy of their enemy; the real question was one of timing. In 1777, the sweeping American victory over Burgoyne at Saratoga, New York, made the French feel that there was a chance England would be defeated after all, and early in 1778, the alliance with the United States was signed.

It is an ironic footnote that if it had not been for the British habit of celebrating long Christmas holidays, the history of the world might have been profoundly altered. Lord Frederick North was a good friend of the American colonies, and a month before Christmas, in 1777, he introduced into Parliament a highly conciliatory bill which gave the North Americans most of what they had asked. But the members of Parliament would not act upon it; they were intent on getting home for the holidays. When they came back on February 17, the bill was passed. Eleven days earlier the alliance with France had been completed, and this news reached America before the report of Lord North's bill. The Americans were in no mood to temporize, and the British effort at conciliation was brushed aside. The real sticking point was that the Revolutionary leaders would not bargain until their independence was recognized, and England was not ready for this.

Secure in his position in the world, Franklin was unruffled under the most trying circumstances. Learning that Edward Gibbon, author of *The Decline and Fall of the Roman Empire,* was in Paris, Franklin wrote him a cordial note inviting him to dinner. Gibbon, never noted for his sense of humor, wrote back stiffly saying he would not break bread with a rebel. Thereupon Ben replied as cordially as before, saying he was sorry, and that when Gibbon came to write *The Decline and Fall of the British Empire,* he would furnish him with a lot of material.

The troubles within the American delegation in Paris remaining as great as ever, Franklin with much tact managed to get Congress to withdraw everyone but himself. Not only did he need to continue the enormously complicated, pressing negotiations with the Court of Louis XVI, but he also was in charge of that part of the naval war with Great Britain conducted in the eastern part of the Atlantic. His best-known action was persuading the French to give him an aged man-of-war, the *Duras,* with forty guns. John Paul Jones, the hyperthyroid ship captain, who had already raided the English and Scottish coasts with startling results, renamed the vessel the *Bonhomme Richard*, in honor of Franklin's Poor Richard.

In September 1779, Jones set out with a handful of small French armed vessels, and soon encountered a British merchant fleet convoyed by two warships, the *Serapis* and the *Countess of Scarborough*. Although the enemy was far stronger than himself, Jones fearlessly attacked. For many hours, the *Bonhomme Richard* and the *Serapis* lay close together, doing dreadful damage to both ships and their crews; when the *Serapis* finally surrendered, the *Bonhomme Richard* was sinking, and Jones transferred to the British vessel to take his prizes into a French court. The French ships that were supposed to help Jones had been worse than useless; the biggest one circled the battle area, firing at the *Bonhomme Richard* quite as often as the *Serapis*.

With the surrender of Cornwallis, it became necessary to write a preliminary peace treaty with England; John Adams came from the Netherlands for this purpose, and John Jay was sent over from the United States. The treaty was signed without the knowledge of the French, since the Americans feared that they would make conditions of their own that would cause a delay the United States could not afford. Franklin had been outvoted on the matter of secrecy, but he loyally made a united front with the other negotiators. With great skill, he played on the psychology of the French leaders and placated them.

In his old age, Franklin suffered from the gout, and he wrote a wonderful "dialogue" with the disease, intended more for others than for himself. In it he gave much good advice in the course of his playful imaginary conversation. The Gout scolded him for playing chess when he should be out walking, and for using his carriage to visit houses that he could have reached on foot. When Ben promises to reform, the Gout observes, "I know you too well. You promise fair; but after a few months of good health, you will return to your old habits."

The reference to chess was a shrewd hit; Franklin adored the game and sometimes sat up all night playing. As usual, he wrote a small book about it which was published and widely read in many countries.

He was equally devoted to playing cards, and felt guilty about it. But then, so he says, he told himself, "You know the soul is immortal; why then should you be such a niggard of a little time when you have a whole eternity before you? . . . Being, like other reasonable creatures, satisfied with a small reason, when it is in favor of doing what I have a mind to do, I shuffle the cards again and begin another game."

Some of his own personal weaknesses proved so unconquerable that he almost reconciled himself to being obliged to go on with them, and confessing this in public reminded him of the man buying an axe who found the sides speckled with a little rust. The seller offered to grind them bright if the buyer would turn the big rotary whetstone. This proved to be hard work and he soon decided he was willing to take the axe as it was. The seller protested, saying, "Turn on, turn on; we shall have it bright bye-and-bye; as yet it is only speckled." To which the buyer replied, "Yes, but I think I like a speckled axe best."

He never hesitated to tell a story at his own

expense. When he was in France and probably the most popular individual in that country, he attended a public ceremony. He could read French readily and spoke it fairly well, but when others spoke rapidly, he found it hard to follow. On this occasion he took his cue from the actions of a woman friend seated near by and applauded heartily whenever she did. Later he learned that he had been cheering eulogies of himself —and louder than anybody.

With his wonderful common sense, Franklin in his mature years always considered in advance the cost of any venture. The most famous of all his essays is the little one illustrating this, called "The Penny Whistle." He tells how as a child of seven, "my friends, on a holiday, filled my pockets with coppers." He went to a shop where he bought a penny whistle, offering all the money he had for it. When he got home, his family

> told me I had given four times as much for it as it was worth; put me in mind what good things I might have bought with the rest of the money, and laughed at me so much for my folly that I cried with vexation; and the reflection gave me more chagrin than the whistle gave me pleasure.

The incident impressed him deeply with the fact that we purchase many things too dearly, and in his essay he lists some who do this. There is the man who neglects his own affairs to court passing favor. There is the miser who to save money gives up "every kind of comfortable living, all the pleasure of doing good to others, all the esteem of his fellow citizens, and the joys of benevolent friendship." There are the wastrel and the show-off; to each of them he says, *You have paid too much for your whistle.*

In Paris he saw the first balloon ascent ever to carry a human being aloft. When a skeptic in the crowd asked what possible use there could ever be for such a device, he countered with a famous question that has been attributed to several other people: What good is a newborn baby? With his power to look ahead, he visualized the possibilities of aerial transportation in peace and, especially, in war, including the rapid transportation of troops to the battlefield or into enemy territory.

In 1785, Franklin at last received permission from the Congress to come back home; he was seventy-nine and suffered severely from a large stone in the bladder. The French could hardly bear to have him go; when he departed from the suburban town of Passy where he had been living, the sedan-chair in which his illness forced him to travel was surrounded by members of his household and by his neighbors, openly weeping. He was followed to his ship, and to America, by affectionate letters from many French friends—the majority, naturally, being from ladies.

News of his coming had preceded him, and Philadelphia made a holiday of his arrival. He was speedily elected "President" (Governor) of the state.

While he was in Europe, the federal authority in America had sunk to a low ebb. The end of the Revolution had brought a slackening to the sense of urgency; there was terrible inflation; the army, not paid for long periods, was on the edge of mutiny. It was clear that a new national government was needed, and in 1786 a Constitutional Convention was called. After a false start, it was held in Philadelphia in 1787.

Washington, the war hero, still the most popular man in America, was there, and so were several of the other great figures of the Revolution—Hamilton, Madison, John Dickinson of Pennsylvania, Gouverneur Morris of New York. Washington set the right tone skillfully at the beginning:

> It is too probable that no plan we propose will be adopted. Perhaps another dreadful conflict is to be sustained [experienced]. If to please the people, we offer what we ourselves disapprove, how can we afterward defend our work? Let us raise a standard to which the wise and the honest can repair; the event is in the hand of God.

Slowly and painfully, with compromise after compromise, the Constitution as we know it today was hammered out, with the ten amendments of the Bill of Rights to follow shortly thereafter. With almost fatal reluctance, the idea was accepted that the states must give up certain powers, and that when there was a conflict between their own and federal law, the latter must prevail.

The Constitution was the work of many men, notable among them James Madison; important emendations were made by Morris, and the actual phraseology was largely from the pen of Edmund Randolph of Virginia. Franklin, though he took little active part in the debate, and seemed to be half asleep much of the time, made some important suggestions about the text. The small states wanted equal representation in Congress, but the big ones, naturally, wished the delegations to be based on population. Franklin helped to bring about the compromise under which the Senate is elected on the first plan, the House on the second.

He also insisted on the right of Congress to impeach a President, remarking that the only alternative in the past had been assassination (a lesson that the twentieth-century dictatorships have had great difficulty in learning). Then Franklin turned around and insisted that there must not be an absolute Presidential veto over the actions of Congress, which would have given the Chief Executive king-like powers.

The Convention had begun on May 14, and the Constitution was signed on September 17. Today it is universally recognized not only as the longest-lived written document of its kind in the world but as one that, on the whole, has worked amazingly well, considering the widely divergent aims of many of the states whose representatives hammered it out.

With much difficulty, including in some cases strong-arm tactics, the Constitution was finally ratified. Franklin, eighty-one and ill, nevertheless played an important part in accomplishing this. Before the Convention ended, he made one of the most important speeches of his career, urging adoption. He admitted that the document was not perfect, but he felt it must be accepted. "There are several parts which I do not at present approve, but I am not sure that I shall never approve them." He had learned in his long life that many positions he had once held had turned out to be wrong. If another Constitutional Convention were to be held, it was not likely to do any better; the new delegates would bring the same prejudices and conflicting interests. On the back of a chair in the hall, a picture of the sun had been painted; Franklin pointed out that a painter cannot indicate whether the orb is rising or setting, and until now he had not been sure which it was. "Now at length I have the happiness to know that it is a rising and not a setting sun."

Though many men argued in favor of the Constitution all over the country, the fact that Franklin and Washington approved of it was probably more effective than anything else in getting it accepted. The proceedings of the Convention were supposed to be secret, but Franklin's speech was smuggled out, and distributed widely through the states, with great effect.

With his work for the Constitution done, Franklin returned to Philadelphia, his public career almost ended. In 1789 he became president of one of the first organizations in America for the abolition of slavery, and he signed, and perhaps wrote, an appeal for money for it. Asked to prepare an inscription for the cornerstone of the new Philadelphia Library, he left his own name off—and the committee in charge promptly wrote it in. He continued to be a scientist to the last, inventing bifocal glasses, and telling his friend, Alexander Small, that he could counteract deafness to some extent, by cupping his hands behind his ears. His bladder stone caused him agony, but he clung to life, hoping to see the new government inaugurated for the country he had served so long and so well.

It was typical of him that toward the end of his life he left a thousand pounds to the city of Philadelphia, and an equal amount to Boston, to be lent to young mechanics who had been apprentices in these cities. But he did not want to make it too easy for them; each borrower was to pay five percent interest and ten percent on the principal each year. (These terms were in fact far below the going rate for interest and amortization in those days.) What he wanted was to help a man to get on his feet and stay there. These funds, greatly augmented through compound interest, are still in existence today.

How he was regarded in those days is indicated in a letter he received a few months after his retirement:

> If the united wishes of a free people, joined with the earnest prayers of every friend to science and humanity, could relieve the body from pain and infirmities, you could claim an exemption on this score . . . If to be venerated for benevolence, to be admired for talent, if to be esteemed for patriotism, if to be beloved for philanthropy, can gratify the human mind, you must have the pleasing consolation to know that you have not lived in vain . . . As long as I retain my memory you will be thought of

with respect, veneration and affection, by, dear Sir, your sincere friend and obedient humble servant,

G. Washington

In 1790, at eighty-four, Franklin died, the most famous private citizen and one of the best-loved public figures in the world. His funeral was the largest ever seen for any person not in office up to that time. The entire French government went into mourning for three days, and Jefferson wanted the American government to do the same. President Washington regretfully said no, not wishing to set a precedent that might later prove embarrassing.

Franklin's career is summed up by Van Doren, who says he was not "one of those men who owe their greatness merely to the opportunities of their time. In any age, in any place, Franklin would have been great. Mind and will, talent and art, strength and ease, wit and grace, met in him as if nature had been lavish and happy when he was shaped."

Many years earlier, when he was still a young man, Franklin had composed his own epitaph, one of the most famous ever written; it has come down to us in several slightly different versions, of which I prefer this one: "The body of B. Franklin, printer, (like the cover of an old book, its contents torn out, and stripped of its lettering and gilding), lies here, food for worms. But the work shall not be wholly lost; for it will [as he believed] appear once more, in a new and more perfect edition, corrected and amended by the Author."

two

John Adams: The Strength of Integrity

AT FIRST glance, nobody could have seemed less like a potential hero. He was short and plump, inclined to pout, egotistical, indiscreet, and with a terrible temper. He was never very tactful, telling people bluntly what he thought, even if it made them enemies, as it often did. He suffered constantly from minor ailments, some of them probably imaginary; although he knew the word *hypochondria,* and applied it to other people, it never occurred to him that it could refer to himself. For all his egoism, he was often afflicted with self-doubt, which he expressed candidly in the pages of the diary that he kept faithfully for many years.

Yet all these weaknesses did not prevent John Adams from being one of the three or four greatest men of the American Revolution. He did fine service in helping France to give the colonies the aid without which the war could not have been won. It was his brilliant mind that realized early that each of the colonies must organize its own state government, and that these must then combine to create a central authority in a republican framework. He was the father of the bicameral legislature, and of the system of checks and balances among the three branches of the federal government, executive, legislative, and judicial.

He negotiated loans in Holland that were essential to the continuance of his virtually bankrupt country. His book on state constitutions helped to steady down the men who had to write them, and to prevent some wild, unsound experimentation that might easily have taken place in the general chaos of the times. Catherine Drinker Bowen, in *John Adams and the American Revolution,* says that he "put a canvas bottom under the American Revolution, so that when the colonies fell, they did not fall through to chaos, bloodshed and a new paternalism."

As one of the American Commissioners in London, he aided in creating the basis for what would have been permanent peace if the British had equalled the Americans in statesmanship. It was he who chose George Washington to lead the army. He founded West Point, established the navy, and stood fast against inflation when many people wanted it. As Vice-President, he prevented war with Great Britain when, presiding over the Senate, he broke a tie vote by deciding for peace. As President, he halted the drift to what might have been an even more disastrous war with France, then in the grip of her own revolution. He did this believing that it would cost him a second term as President—and he was right. All his life long he was famous for his scrupulous, unbending honesty.

In an age of brilliant pamphleteers, he was one of the best. By his writings he played a great part in welding into a nation the separate colonies which at the beginning had no real government, had widely conflicting interests, were jealous and suspicious, and were in every case deeply divided internally over the question of breaking away from Great Britain. Time and time again, at critical points, he made speeches, most of them in meetings of the Continental Congress, that resulted in the right decisions.

The portraits of him that survive show a man short and stocky, with a round, plump face, a jutting nose, inquisitive eyes, and firm compressed lips. He wore his hair long, in the fashion of the day (in some portraits he may have been wearing a wig), with the ends, which hung down covering his ears, slightly rolled. In middle life he was bald in front and eventually the bald area covered the top of his head.

The nickname by which he was known for years, "Old Sink or Swim," came from a famous letter he had written to a man who was once his dearest friend, Jonathan Sewall. Jonathan tried, when the tension was highest, to persuade John to become a Tory, as he himself had done. John wrote refusing, saying, "I have passed my Rubicon. I will never change. Sink or swim, live or die, survive or perish, I am with my country from this day on."

In general, he was an excellent propagandist for the cause of the colonials. In 1775 he felt the need to restate their case against the mother country in full. At home in Braintree, pacing up and down, and dictating to Abigail in a torrent of words, he poured out what was in his heart. England had made no effort to create a plan for government in America. She had violated both the rights of the colonials under English law and their inherent rights as human beings. The book was published that same year both in America and in England, under the title *History of the Dispute in America from Its Origin in 1754 to the Present Time*, and got wide attention.

John Adams was born October 30, 1735, in Braintree. His father, a farmer, was a man of some learning, respected in his community. John grew up on the farm, sharing from an early age in the work that needed to be done, as far as a boy's strength would permit. His childhood was lived under the shadow of the French and Indian Wars, which had begun in 1689, paralleling the European War of the General Alliance, and did not end until the decisive defeat of the French in 1760, following the British capture of

Quebec; the struggle in America was by now a phase of the Seven Years' War in Europe.

As a boy, John was sent to an inferior school in Braintree, hated it, and did poorly in his studies. At an early age he asked to be taken out of this school and allowed to work on the farm. His father, trying to change his mind, worked him hard, but the boy was as stubborn as he was to be for the rest of his life. There was another school in the town, and on his own initiative, John enrolled in it. He did much better and was soon planning for Harvard, which he entered at fifteen, an age much less unusual then than it would be today.

Harvard was still conducted in the Puritan tradition, with heavy emphasis on religion, Greek, and Latin. Instruction in science was in its infancy, and there were few other subjects in the curriculum. The students lived with great austerity. They were fined five shillings if they were caught telling a lie, entering a saloon, fighting with each other, swearing, disturbing their classmates with noise, or getting drunk. The fine for being caught playing with cards or gambling with dice was four times as large.

While the number of subjects taught was small, the teaching was thorough. Repeatedly we find, among college men of that day whose records have come down to us, that they could readily read and write Greek and Latin, and did so all their days. They learned to love books, and the leaders among them, at any rate, were trained to pursue knowledge eagerly.

In college, Adams was not aware that the subjects of study were few. On the contrary, in the sections of his diary unearthed in 1965, he reported that "I have so many irons in the fire that every one burns. I have common, civil [and] natural law, poetry, oratory, in Greek, Latin, French, English, to study, so that when I set down [sic] to read or think, so many subjects rush into my mind that I know not which to choose."

John joined the Harvard Discussion Club, whose members practiced public speaking, or sometimes read aloud books and plays. A recent law had made the theater illegal in the colony, but the students circumvented this by calling a play a "dramatic composition." Since they did not charge admission, or let in anyone not a member, the authorities would presumably have ignored them.

In this club, John spoke in public for the first time, something he would spend the rest of his life doing. His assignment was not a speech, but a memorized passage from a play. One of his biographers, Catherine Bowen, reports that he had such stage fright he was unable to open his mouth. Furious, he practiced for weeks on another speech from a play; this was Shakespeare's *Coriolanus*. It was performed well, and was applauded.

Though Harvard taught little physical science, Adams, like other great men of his day, had broad interest in many scientific matters. His diary contains references to chemistry, physics, mathematics, lightning, experiments with steam engines, geology, marine biology, medicine, oceanography, archaeology, and ship architecture.

The family had taken it for granted that John would become a minister, but to their great disappointment, he decided against it. While he was still trying to choose a profession, he was offered a job teaching school in Worcester, and postponed the decision by accepting temporarily.

He finally decided to follow the law, perhaps because he had made the acquaintance of John Putnam, a leading Worcester attorney. Practicing law as a means of supporting oneself was fairly new in Massachusetts; only fifty years earlier a law had been repealed forbidding anyone to accept money for representing a client. There were no law schools or bar examinations; you "read law" in the office of an attorney, and when this man thought you were qualified, he introduced you to the legal community. In the absence of any opposition, you were now a member of the bar. With some setbacks, John achieved this.

His merit in practice soon became apparent, and the demand for his services rapidly grew. He was one of the first Americans to read and thoroughly digest the famous work of Sir William Blackstone, *An Analysis of the Laws of England,* and since the American colonies were under British law, it stood him in good stead. All his life he had a lawyer's trick of going back to the fundamentals of the statutes, and the "natural law" which underlay them, to get into its proper frame of reference any cause he had to plead. After a beginning in Braintree his practice was before long so large that he had to move to Boston.

He knew how to use some effective devices in the courtroom. The British were kidnapping sailors from American ships and forcing them to serve in the

English navy; on one occasion some of them resisted, in the struggle a British naval officer was killed, and four of the Americans were brought to Boston and tried for murder. John, defending them, entered the courtroom at the beginning of the trial, carrying a large book, sat down a few feet from the judges and conspicuously opened it and laid it on his table. The judges precipitously got up and left the room to confer in their chambers, coming back shortly to rule that the four defendants were not guilty, having acted in self-defense. The book John had brought in was the British *Statutes at Large*, probably the only copy in private hands in America at that time. He had opened it, as the judges could plainly see, to the page containing a law forbidding the kidnapping of American sailors.

As soon as the British perceived that he was one of the coming men of Massachusetts, they tried to bring him over to their side. He was offered the job of King's Advocate in the Admiralty Court, which would have meant permanent security, a big salary, and the probability of becoming Chief Justice. He unceremoniously refused.

Long before this, he had married. Abigail Smith, daughter of a minister in the nearby town of Weymouth, was a brilliant girl, who could read philosophical books quite as abstruse as those John perused, and she chafed for many years because women in that day were not supposed to be intellectual. Though he probably would have done so in any case, John felt somewhat more free to marry because his father had died and he had inherited thirty acres of land and one of the family's two houses.

The marriage took place in 1764, when John was twenty-nine and Abigail was twenty. Abigail was as remarkable in her own way as John was in his. She was by far the most brilliant of the wives of the great heroes of the Revolution, and in all probability, the only one who could have played a role beyond that of wife and mother. She was an invaluable correspondent, reporting to him not only on the fluctuating winds of political opinion in Massachusetts but even, when the British were still occupying Boston and a species of guerrilla warfare was in progress, on military matters. For the first few years of his government service, Adams, like the other congressmen, received no salary and only very modest expense money, paid by Massachusetts. Abigail supported herself and her children by working the farm, originally thirty acres, some of which was marshland unfit for use. While John complained constantly to her, she rarely responded in kind. He gave her a warning that she certainly did not need, that the coming revolution would mean hard times. "Frugality, my dear, frugality, economy, parsimony, must be our refuge . . . Let us eat potatoes and drink water. Let us wear canvas and undressed sheepskins, rather than submit to the unrighteous and ignominious domination that is prepared for us."

If we can judge by the letters, she had more wit than he, great native sagacity, and a strong fund of common sense, useful to steady down a husband who could fly off the handle on slight provocation.

John had a profound belief in the value of schooling. "Education," he wrote, "makes a greater difference between man and man than nature has made between man and brute. The virtues and powers to which men may be trained, by early education and constant discipline, are truly sublime and astonishing." When the children were little, Adams was greatly concerned about their upbringing, and filled his letters with admonitions to Abigail, and sometimes to the children themselves, about the cultivation of good habits:

> The education of our children is never out of my mind. Train them to virtue. Habituate them to industry, activity and spirit. Make them consider every vice as shameful and unmanly. Fire them with ambition to be useful. Make them disdain to be destitute of any useful or ornamental knowledge or accomplishment. Fix their ambition upon great and solid objects and their contempt upon little, frivolous and useless ones. Every decency, grace and honesty should be inculcated upon them.

How effective all this advice was is doubtful. To be sure, one of his sons, John Quincy Adams, became the sixth President of the United States, a member of the only father-and-son team in our history to achieve that office. But none of his other children achieved any sort of fame and one of them, Charles, met an early death as an alcoholic.

The rigorous discipline he wanted imposed on his children paralleled the equally drastic regimen he imposed on himself as a young man. Like Franklin, he laid out a course of daily studies for himself that would have required heroism, if he had stuck to it very long. He confided to his diary that he planned to get up before sunrise, read various volumes of law until ten o'clock, and from ten o'clock until noon to read laws relating to naval affairs. After his noon dinner, he would walk out of doors to keep himself healthy. In the evenings he would go back to reading, in the fields of philosophy and history.

John Adams was a dedicated and prolific writer but a careless man, who made many errors through haste and a faulty memory. The first part of his autobiography, which he began in 1802, after he had retired from the Presidency, seems to have been written almost entirely from his not very accurate memory; then he remembered that the diary existed and not only used it as source material, but copied long passages verbatim.

If he had written nothing else than the diary and the autobiography, these two works would secure for him a place in history. He never failed to be clear, simple, unpretentious, and direct. He gives in the diary a straightforward, pithy, and comprehensive account of all that happened to him, where he went, and whom he met. As might be expected, he writes many comments on his contemporaries, rarely erring on the side of discretion.

In many cases, especially when he was young, Adams began a day's record with a word or two of what had happened and then plunged immediately into philosophizing. Here are two or three examples taken at random from the spring of 1756, before he was twenty-one:

Drank tea at Mr. Putnam's.—What is the proper business of mankind in this life? We come into the world naked and destitute of all the conveniences and necessaries of life. And if we were not provided for and nourished by our parents or others should inevitably perish as soon as born . . . If we live to the age of three score and ten and then set down to make an estimate in our minds of the happiness we have enjoyed and the misery we have suffered, we shall find, I am apt to think, that the overbalance of happiness is quite inconsiderable. We shall find that . . . we have applied our whole vigor, all our faculties, in the pursuit of honor, or wealth, or learning, or some other such delusive trifle, instead of the real and everlasting excellences of piety and virtue . . .

Drank tea at the Major's.—The reason of mathematicians is founded on certain and infallible principles. Every word they use conveys a determinate idea and by accurate definitions they excite the same ideas in the mind of the reader that were in the mind of the writer . . . They take for granted certain postulates . . . and from these plain, simple principles, they have raised most astonishing speculations, and proved the extent of the human mind to be more spacious and capable than any other science.

Went to Spencer in the afternoon.—When we come into the world our minds are destitute of all sorts of ideas. Our senses inform us of various qualities in the substances around us . . . We can modify and dispose the simple ideas of sensation into whatever shape we please. But these ideas can enter our minds no other way but through the senses.

All his life long, he was to pour out his philosophy, in his diary, his letters, his speeches and state papers. A recurring theme was the importance of maintaining freedom.

Cities may be rebuilt, and a people, reduced to poverty, may acquire fresh property, but a constitution of government, once changed from freedom, can never be restored. Liberty, once lost, is lost forever. When the people once surrender their share in the legislature and their rights of defending the limitations upon the Government, and of resisting every encroachment upon them, they can never regain it.

Sometimes he seems to be admonishing himself rather than others. In 1774, he wrote that he feared Congress would not do what needed to be done, but then tried to cheer himself up. "Vapors avaunt! I will do my duty and leave the event. If I have the approbation of my own mind, whether applauded or censured, blessed or cursed, by the world, I will not be unhappy."

This man, one of the most ambitious who ever lived, recognized that this could be a fault:

I believe there is no one principle which predominates in human nature so much . . . as

> the passion for superiority. Every human being compares itself in its imagination with every other round about it, and will find some superiority over other, real or imaginary, or it will die of grief and vexation.

He knew that the tendency to quarrel was a handicap. In 1774, he reported, "It has long been my resolution to avoid . . . all passion and personal altercation or reflections. I have found it difficult to keep these resolutions exactly," which was certainly an understatement. He thought, however, that he had been doing pretty well for the past six years.

He was troubled, like many another man before and since, to know why God permits evil to exist, and decided He does so "because [not to do so] would destroy the liberty without which there could be no moral good or evil in the universe." Otherwise life would be "a mere chemical process, a mere mechanical engine to produce nothing but pleasure." He did not think man could ever be made perfect, but we should try.

His diary faithfully recorded his weaknesses as well as his resolve to overcome them:

> I can as easily still the tempest or stop the rapid thunderbolt as command the motions and operations of my own mind. My brain seems constantly in as great confusion and wild disorder as Milton's chaos. Vanity, I am sensible, is my cardinal vice and folly . . . I never have any bright, refulgent ideas. Everything appears in my mind dim and obscure,

> like objects seen through a dirty glass or roiled water.

In his old age he took a different view of the vanity with which he had been reproached for so many years.

> They say I am vain. Thank God I am so. Vanity is the cordial drop which makes the bitter cup of life go down.

But in his youth this acceptance of weakness was far from his mind. "May I blush," he told his diary, "whenever I suffer one hour to pass unimproved."

> I will rouse up my mind and fix my attention; I will stand collected within myself and think upon what I read and what I see. I will strive with all my soul to be something more than persons who have had less advantages than myself.

Already he knew that his sharp and indiscreet tongue might get him into trouble.

> I now resolve for the future never to say an ill-natured or an envious thing concerning governors, judges, ministers, sheriffs, lawyers or any honorable or lucrative offices or officers . . . Now let me collect my thoughts. Now let me form great habits of thinking, writing, speaking. Let love and vanity be extinguished, and the great passions of ambition [and] patri-

> otism break out and burn. Let little objects be neglected and forgot, and great ones engross and exalt my soul.

He did indeed spend much of his life busy with great thoughts and deeds, but his resolution to speak ill of no one he violated many times. He wrote harshly of his colleagues, and once tossed in a bit of important military information. This letter was captured by the Tories, published on both sides of the Atlantic, and caused great indignation. The episode would have ruined a less important person, but he was able to brazen it out.

John and Abigail were happy together, but the first decade of their life in Braintree was clouded by trouble between the colonies and the mother country. The repeated restrictions on American trade were intended both to hamper colonial businessmen in favor of those of England and to raise revenue for the home government. Two-thirds of a century earlier, in 1699, London had ruled that American woolen goods could not be transported between colonies by water; this was at a time when there were few good roads and overland transportation was most difficult, except in winter, and then only in the northern part of the country, when sleds could be used on the snow. In 1732, when a flourishing industry in making hats had grown up, their export was flatly forbidden.

In 1750, the pressure had been increased again. All manufacture of iron products in the colonies was forbidden, even horseshoes and nails. This law, also, was widely circumvented, but it helped to exacerbate relations.

I have reported earlier the furious uproar created throughout all the colonies by the Stamp Act of 1765, designed to raise £60,000 a year. Adams, by now the leading lawyer of Massachusetts, was called upon, with hardly any time for preparation, to appear before the Governor to argue against the Act. He made a legalistic argument, as did two other men who appeared with him. Their chief charge was one that was to become famous, that taxation without representation was contrary to the spirit of Magna Carta. The Governor dodged the issue by referring the question to the courts; eventually, as already recorded, the Stamp Act was repealed, thanks largely to the magnificent work of Franklin in London.

Proving that it had learned nothing, a little later the British government passed the Townshend Act of 1767, which levied taxes on glass, paper, printers' lead, and tea. Again there was fury against England throughout the colonies. In 1770 three of these taxes were canceled but the one on tea was retained; and the inhabitants of the British colonies were tea drinkers to the last man.

There had been riots in Boston five years earlier when the Stamp Act was passed, and so much trouble ever since that the British had stationed troops in Boston to keep order. There were scores of minor clashes, and on March 5, 1770, occurred the incident that America has ever since described as the Boston Massacre. A British sentry on duty was faced by a furious mob who threw sticks, stones, and heavy pieces of ice at him. He quite naturally shouted for help, and a file of eight more soldiers and Capt. Thomas Preston turned out to aid him. The abuse from the crowd and the throwing of missiles continued. Thereupon, after efforts to persuade the crowd to disperse, Captain Preston ordered his men to fire, at point-blank range. Three were killed and eight were wounded, two of them subsequently dying. Captain Preston and the soldiers were promptly arrested, charged with murder.

Who would defend them? Feeling ran so high in the colony that anyone who undertook to do so was in serious danger. Nevertheless, when James Forrest, a prominent Tory, asked him to appear, Adams instantly agreed. Forrest gave him one guinea as a retainer, and eventually he was paid another eighteen guineas, for services that would customarily have been worth many times more. He records the payments in his autobiography (in his diary at the time he made no mention of the whole affair), because people had spread stories that he had received a gigantic fee for what many regarded as virtually an act of treason to Massachusetts.

The first thing Adams and Josiah Quincy, Jr., who served with him, did was to get a delay of several months to let Boston cool off. Then Captain Preston, who had given the order to fire but had not himself used a musket, was tried and set free. With great skill Adams riddled the testimony of scores of perjured witnesses, who tried to show that the soldiers had fired without provocation; he proved, on the contrary, that their lives had been in danger, and appealed to the feelings for fair play and law and order which continued in Massachusetts, even if the mother country had forgotten them. After Preston was found innocent, so were six of eight soldiers. Two of them were found guilty of manslaughter, and immediately asked for "benefit of clergy." Invoking this phrase was a curious legal device that went back to the Middle Ages, and consisted originally of proving you could read and write; in the twilit centuries, this created an automatic assumption that you were a monk. Benefit of clergy was granted the two British soldiers, and each was branded on the thumb with a hot iron—painful, but preferable to the noose—and set free.

John, aged thirty-five, was sure that he had ruined himself politically, and accepted his retirement as gracefully as he could. "[Henceforth] I divide my time between law and husbandry," he wrote a little later. "Farewell, politics!" His farewell was somewhat premature.

Even while the echoes of the British soldiers' trial were still ringing, he had been overwhelmingly elected to the Massachusetts State Legislature. Despite all the scandalous gossip about him, a majority of his fellow citizens recognized that he was acting in the best tradition of British institutions and of the law.

Through the first half of the 1770s, tension steadily mounted between the mother country and the colonies. The chief centers of protest were Massachusetts, with its large artisan population, and Virginia, where the wealthy plantation owners chafed under the restrictions imposed by London on their trade. When a British orator referred contemptuously to "the sons of liberty" in Massachusetts, the agitators there picked up the phrase and wore it proudly.

London, seeking to break the boycott (a word that did not come into use until a century later) on tea, cut the price drastically, and authorized the East India Company to send its ships directly from Asia to American ports. The tax of threepence a pound was not reduced, however, and there was a real attempt to stop smuggling. Now occurred the famous Boston Tea Party; a band of Sons of Liberty, dressed as Indians with painted faces (to avoid recognition) boarded the ships and threw overboard tea worth about £18,000—several times the value of the same sum today.

Within a few months, London struck back with a complete embargo on trade by sea with Boston until the tea was paid for; other colonies, which had refused but not destroyed the tea, were not punished so severely. Paul Revere, a good horseman as well as a good silversmith, rode south with letters asking help for beleaguered Boston, and several colonies sent her food and other necessities. Old Israel Putnam of Connecticut, a veteran of the French and Indian Wars, donated 130 sheep—and himself drove them to Boston, nearly a hundred miles.

Things at last got bad enough to necessitate the calling of the First Continental Congress, to meet in Philadelphia on December 5, 1774. That John Adams, now one of the two or three leading citizens of Massachusetts, would be one of that colony's delegates was a foregone conclusion. The colony voted £500 for the delegates' expenses.

It is hard for us to realize today how deeply the colonies were still divided and on how many issues. The South was an area of big plantations, many slaves, few manufactures. Maryland was heavily populated with Roman Catholics; Protestant New England was bitterly opposed to them. Massachusetts was comparatively industrialized, even though the great majority of its people earned their living from the soil; it had many artisans with what might even then be called a working-class psychology, and there were few slaves. New York was dominated by the conservative descendants of the rich Dutch patroons, who had been granted big estates up the Hudson. Pennsylvania had many Quakers who were pacifists and reluctant for several reasons to antagonize London.

Many of the delegates still believed that if they could only petition the King with sufficient urgency he would change the regulations that were hurting the colonies. The radicals, among whom Sam Adams, John's second cousin, was a leader, wanted to cut off trade with Great Britain even more completely than in the past, break the British blockade of Boston by force, and change the whole system of taxation. They had to walk gingerly for fear they would alienate the moderates who would then reject their whole program.

The chaos of that first Congress may be judged from the question John Adams immediately raised: What was to be the basis for voting? One vote for each delegate? Or one for each colony? The colonies varied greatly in population, and since no limit had been put on the number of delegates each could send, these also varied. In this dilemma, John Jay proposed a temporary solution, one vote to each colony; like so many temporary actions of deliberative bodies, this turned out to be permanent.

Most of the time for the next eighteen months, the First and Second Continental Congresses worked hard trying to bring some order out of the confusion of their improvised organization. The impatient Adams felt, however, that they talked too much, and that too many men insisted on being heard on every subject. "I believe, if it was moved and seconded that we should come to a resolution that three and two makes five, we should be entertained with logic and rhetoric, law, history, politics and mathematics, and then—we should pass the resolution unanimously in the affirmative."

The Congress had begun by creating two large committees, one to draw up a statement of the rights and grievances of the colonies, the other to try to hammer out policies on trade and taxation. The writing of a formal document justifying the existence of the Congress presented numerous difficulties. How much authority should they admit that the British Parliament was to exercise in the future? The Congress came to a dead halt until John Adams solved it for them with a single sentence: "Deny Parliament's authority as a matter of right but consent to it as a matter of necessity."

While the Congress worked long hours, events moved ahead without waiting for them. The break between the Massachusetts Legislature and the Royal Governor became complete; the Legislature refused to dissolve as he ordered, and instead moved out of Boston and continued its business; thus British rule in

Massachusetts came to an end forever. When the Continental Congress was less than four months old, Patrick Henry made a stirring address to the Revolutionary Convention in Richmond, Virginia, on March 23, 1775, concluding with, "Give me liberty or give me death." Soon thereafter occurred the battle of Lexington, from which the British retreated in some disorder. Less than a month later, American troops headed by two brilliant commanders, Ethan Allen and Benedict Arnold, boldly captured Fort Ticonderoga, at the head of Lake George, which was held by the British.

John Adams was responsible for one of the most important acts of the entire era when he persuaded the Continental Congress, on June 15, 1775, to name George Washington Commander in Chief of the Congress forces. Washington, a colonel of the Virginia militia, had told the colony's House of Burgesses, "If need be, I will raise a thousand men, subsist them at my own expense, and march, myself at their head, to the relief of Boston." His appointment was a political master stroke; by putting a Virginian at the head of troops in Massachusetts, the spot where fighting was going on, the unity of the colonies was emphasized.

Washington at once prepared to leave for Massachusetts. He had only started, however, when news came of a battle in Boston. It occurred on Breed's Hill, but since the patriots had intended to fortify Bunker Hill, and got the wrong one by mistake, it is called the battle of Bunker Hill. The British took it, but at heavy cost in casualties. Most of the Americans got away.

When Washington arrived in Cambridge, the headquarters of the patriots, he was confronted by the desperate situation that was to be repeated almost to the very end of the war. His army consisted of volunteers who had been jolted out of their complacency, if they had any, by the continued intransigence of the British. They had no uniforms, few arms, and little ammunition; as a rule, each man came wearing his own clothes and bringing his own musket, powder, and bullets—if he had any. Some of them Washington had to arm temporarily with spears! Their enlistments were for a short period, and most of them planned to go home when their time was up.

Washington's difficult position was paralleled by the problems with which the Congress, in Philadelphia, was confronted, obliged to support a war for which it was almost totally unprepared. It had to provide munitions, supplies of every sort, hospitals, doctors, nurses, medicine. Communication was now so important that the post office had to be expanded. In the hope of keeping the Indians neutral, a Department of Indian Affairs was set up.

In this dark time, there were two items of good news. Georgia now came in, increasing the number of colonies represented from twelve to thirteen. Col. Henry Knox, a Boston bookseller turned soldier, managed to drag more than fifty cannon, mortars and howitzers, from Ticonderoga and nearby Crown Point two hundred miles through the wilderness to the Boston area. Washington was overjoyed; in a single night he managed to fortify Dorchester Heights, overlooking the harbor where the British men-of-war lay at anchor. When dawn came, the Redcoats saw the bristling guns and realized their situation was untenable. Promptly they evacuated Boston and sailed away, taking with them some hundreds of well-known Tory sympathizers.

By the spring of 1776 the mood of the colonies had darkened as they saw more and more clearly that England did not intend to offer any sort of viable compromise. Yet tradition died hard. Congress inched its way toward a final break with the mother country, with John Adams in the forefront of the movement. Finally, it appointed a committee of five to write a Declaration of Independence.

On July 1, 1776, Adams made the most important speech of his whole life. No text has survived, but John himself summarized it later. John Dickinson had talked at great length, arguing against independence; Adams waited for someone to answer him, but since no one did, he himself rose and recited the reasons why a complete break was necessary. Said one of the delegates, Richard Stockton of New Jersey, long afterward:

> The man to whom the country is most indebted for the great measure of independence is Mr. John Adams of Boston. I call him the Atlas of American independence. He it was who sustained the debate, and by the force of his reasoning demonstrated not only the justice but the expediency of the measure.

On July 2, Congress formally voted to accept the principle of independence, and on July 4, it adopted the Declaration, almost entirely the work of Jefferson.

If there were some who did not realize the momentous character of these events, Adams was not among them. On July 3, after the principle had been adopted, but before Jefferson's text had been made official, he wrote to Abigail.

> Yesterday the greatest question was decided which ever was debated in America, and a greater, perhaps, never was nor will be decided among men. A Resolution was passed without one dissenting colony "that these United Colonies are, and of right ought to be, free and independent states and as such they have, and of right ought to have, full power to make war, conclude peace, establish commerce, and to do all other acts and things which other states may rightfully do." You will see in a few days a Declaration setting forth the causes which have impelled us to this mighty revolution, and the reasons which will justify it in the sight of God and man. A plan of Confederation will be taken up in a few days.
>
> . . . I am surprised at the suddenness as well as the greatness of this revolution. Britain has been filled with folly and America with wisdom; at least this is my judgment; time must determine. It is the will of Heaven that the two countries should be sundered forever. It may be the will of Heaven that America shall suffer calamities still more wasting and distresses yet more dreadful. If this is to be the case, it will have this good effect at least: It will inspire us with many virtues which we have not, and

> correct many errors, follies and vices which threaten to disturb, dishonor and destroy us.

Six months earlier he had expressed his sense of the importance of the times and of the privilege in participating in what was happening. In January he wrote to a fellow member of Congress:

> You and I have been sent into life at a time when the greatest lawgivers of antiquity would have wished to live. When, before the present [epoch], had three millions of people full power and a fair opportunity to form and establish the wisest and happiest government that human wisdom can contrive?

He knew that the events of that July had been a long time in the making. Nearly forty years later, when he was eighty, he wrote:

> What do they mean by the Revolution? The war with Britain? That was no part of the Revolution; it was only the effect and consequence of it. The Revolution was in the minds and hearts of the people and this was effected from 1760 to 1775, in the course of fifteen years, before a drop of blood was shed at Lexington.

The war had of course begun some fifteen months before the Continental Congress voted for independence, and its members during that time had been heavily burdened with work; but now their duties were redoubled. They had to improvise a government for a new country. Every day, actions must be taken for which they had no precedent. There was long debate during the next months, before the Articles of Confederation and Perpetual Union were adopted (but not ratified) in November of 1777. Should Virginia be allowed to extend her boundaries, as she wished, to the Pacific Ocean? What should be done about states that were trying to take territory from one another, as Connecticut and Virginia were both trying to do to Pennsylvania? It was desperately urgent to try to switch the allegiance of some Indian tribes from Great Britain to the Congress, and to persuade others to remain neutral.

A bitter dispute developed over the basis of voting in the Congress, which for two years had gone on the "temporary basis" of one colony, one vote. If the states were not to continue this, should the basis be population, favored by the big states, opposed by the small ones? Or property? And if the latter, were Negro slaves property, as the South affirmed and the North denied? By a narrow vote, it was decided that Negroes are people, after a fight that threatened to destroy the shaky Union.

No member of the Congress worked harder than John Adams. He was now Chairman of the Board of War, the equivalent of today's Secretary of War, with enormous burdens on his shoulders. He complained that the army did not keep him informed, and Congress did not take his advice. Everything you can name was in short supply—guns, ammunition, clothing. The privates in the ranks showed a degree of independence that would be breathtaking today. When their period of enlistment was up, many of them simply elected to go home, taking their weapons with them, and there was nobody to stop them. New England soldiers would fight only under officers of their own choosing, usually men from their own region. Of an army supposed to be twenty-five thousand strong, only seventeen thousand were fit for duty. So many officers wrote to Congress complaining bitterly of their low pay, that this was finally raised; a colonel was now to get the staggering sum of $75 a month, a lieutenant $27. The Congress was always out of money; it had to float loans, and these were at rates of interest that increased as the difficulties of the war became more evident.

On top of all his other troubles, Adams' eyes were bad. Also, he greatly missed his favorite old form of exercise, riding horseback, and finally, when he was about to return briefly to Massachusetts, begged Abigail to send him a horse; he did not think he could endure another jolting ride by coach from Philadelphia to Braintree.

Yet he refused to be pessimistic. "Patience and perseverance," he wrote, "will carry us through this mighty enterprise—an enterprise that is and will be an astonishment to vulgar minds all over the world in this and future generations." He yearned for his home more than ever. "Happy would I be indeed," he said in a letter to Abigail, "if I could share with you in the products of your little farm. Milk and apples and pork and beef and the fruits of the garden would be luxury to me." He was too poor to buy wine, though he did not miss it greatly. His family had plain food from the farm, as he knew, but no sugar, molasses, coffee, or chocolate, items which commanded soaring prices on the black market. Adams seriously considered trying to spend only half a year in Philadelphia and the other half earning money in Boston; but he knew this was impractical. He presently resigned a post to which he had been elected, as Chief Justice of Massachusetts, a position he had never had time to fill.

The Board of War in these days usually met at 6 A.M., and continued in session until its members had to join the rest of the Congress at noon; or sometimes it would meet after Congress had adjourned and labor far into the night. Yet John managed to write regularly to his family. John Quincy, now nine years old, rode to Boston from time to time for the accumulated mail; he teased his mother by doling out John's letters to her one by one, pretending in each case that it was the last. John wrote to each of the children except Tommy, who was too young to read; when Tommy burst into tears over this discrimination, Abigail gave him one of hers, assuring him that it was his own. Informed of this, John immediately wrote an authentic letter for Tommy which Abigail read aloud to him.

While the Congress worked in a fever in Philadelphia, great events were happening elsewhere. Washington was forced to yield New York and to retreat toward the South. On the day after Christmas, he achieved one of the first substantial American successes of the war when he crossed the ice-clogged Delaware River and captured Trenton from the German mercenaries, many of whom had rashly celebrated Christmas with too much rum and were not in very good shape to fight.

In September of 1777, the war suddenly came home to the Congress when in the dead of night its members had to be routed out of bed and forced to flee from Philadelphia because General Howe was on the point of capturing the city. One town after another became the temporary capital—Lancaster and York, Pennsylvania, and Baltimore, Maryland. Yet the members went on doing business; only about two months later, the Articles of Confederation were agreed upon, to come into effect with the end of the war.

But now, Adams was to be suddenly transported from this scene; the Congress voted to send him to France to help Ben Franklin in the desperately important effort to improve relations with the government of Louis XVI.

The next ten years were the most frustrating of Adams' life. As a member of Congress he had been at the heart of American power, giving orders for others to execute, almost instantly informed (despite his complaints about Congress and the army) of everything important that was going on. Now he was soon to find himself taking orders, and taking them, moreover, from a distant authority that was extraordinarily careless about answering letters, and even at the best required up to three months for a reply.

The voyage over was a wretched one, as all his voyages were to be. The crew was badly disciplined, and the ship was filthy until Adams, by sheer power of character, compelled the captain to clean it up. There was a terrible storm for three days, and he was violently seasick. The ship was chased by two British vessels; Adams wanted to stop and fight them, but the captain sensibly elected to escape under cover of the weather.

When he finally arrived, Paris had an enormous impact on the provincial Bostonian. He marveled at the beauty of the buildings, the wealth of art displayed on every hand, the sophistication and culture of the inhabitants. He was impressed by the fact that the women joined in the discussion of every subject on an equal basis with the men. He wrote to Abigail that it would take several generations for America to reach an equal cultural development, since so much must first be done in the fields of politics and economics. Yet as time went on, Adams was shocked by what he considered the loose moral standards of the French. The man from Puritan New England blushed at the salty character of the conversation, even in the best drawing rooms.

I have already reported the difficulties of the American delegation in Paris, where the attitude of the French fluctuated with the success of the Revolutionary arms in America. Inevitably Adams disapproved of Franklin, who seemed so lazy and so incorrigibly fond of the ladies. The Bostonian could not comprehend the subtle and skillful political game Franklin was playing and was bewildered when he discovered how effective it had been. John was happy to come home in the summer of 1779, arriving in Boston on August 2, after a voyage of more than six weeks.

As it turned out, he was to spend only a few months at home before Congress sent him back to Paris. Those few months, however, were of great importance, because during them he drafted a new Constitution for Massachusetts, emphasizing the all-important division of the government into three equal branches, legislative, executive, and judicial. This system was to be copied when the federal Constitution came to be written eight years later.

Back in Europe, Adams continued to be unhappy for several reasons. His health was often poor, and the uxorious man from Braintree missed his wife and children terribly. He kept pleading with Abigail to come over, but with a farm on her hands, and a houseful of young children, she did not see how this was possible, though she finally made the trip in 1784, five years later. In the meantime she had been so hard up that she begged him to send her French trinkets of various kinds that she could sell, to put a little money into her purse.

Adams was enormously useful to his country during this period. The best financial source for the United States in Europe was the rich bankers of the Netherlands, and he was sent there to raise money. In the next few years, he floated four successive loans. The Dutch were hard bargainers and demanded high rates, which America was forced to pay. Adams had a terrible time getting them to recognize him as the legal American Minister, and finally achieved this only by sheer force of character. In the Netherlands he had the most serious illness of his life, a protracted fever; he believed that he felt its effects for the rest of his days. With great efforts, he finally, early in 1782, got recognition as Minister Plenipotentiary, and signed a treaty of amity and commerce.

His illness made him despondent, as happened more than once in his life. A few months later he reported in a letter that he was now a broken old man, and proposed to spend the feeble remnants of his life as a farmer. He was forty-seven.

When the fighting ended, there was still much to be done: the preliminary peace treaty with Great Britain, the final one, and a supplementary commercial agreement. When he went to London, in October 1783, accompanied by John Jay, the atmosphere was so hostile that at first the two Americans felt they could only mark time until British tempers had cooled a little. Adams was helped by the friendship of Lord Mansfield—the same Lord Mansfield who had warned the House of Lords about him while the war was still in progress, "My Lords, if you do not kill him, he will kill you."

In 1784, things brightened for John enormously because Abigail, leaving the younger children with friends, came over to be with him (the two eldest boys were already with their father). Her voyage across was as miserable as were all others in those days. She took a cow on board, but in a bad storm it was injured and had to be killed. Abigail herself was terribly seasick for a time, but soon recovered and with characteristic energy, she had the filthy ship cleaned up from stem to stern, as a proper New England housewife would do. The ship's cook was grossly incompetent, so she taught him the rudiments of his profession.

In 1785, John was elected the first American Minister to the British Court, and he and Abigail took up residence in London. The Congress, with its usual parsimony, paid John so meagerly that his skimped standard of living was the source of ribald jokes among the English. Mrs. Adams, market basket over arm, sallied forth daily to do her own marketing, at a time when English ladies of equivalent status would never dream of doing such a thing. The Adamses had no choice, and put the best face they could on their predicament.

Brought up in a rather egalitarian society, Abigail Adams hated the snobbery of London, and the ridicule which was directed against her because the American Minister was so poor that his wife had to do her own shopping. Nevertheless, John was fairly happy during the four years that he and Abigail spent in London. They had little occasion to write each other letters, but when they did, he frolicked like a schoolboy. A fair example is a letter he wrote her on Christmas Day, 1786, when she had gone to Bath for a short visit, and he was forced to stay in London.

> If I am cold in the night and an additional quantity of bedclothes will not answer the purpose of warming me, I will take a virgin to bed with me. Ay! a virgin.
>
> What? Oh! Awful! What do I read?
>
> Don't be surprised. Do you know what a virgin is? Mr. Bridgen [made me] acquainted with it this morning. It is a stone bottle . . . filled with boiling water, covered over or wrapped up in flannel, and laid at a man's feet in bed. An old man, you see, may comfort him-

> self with such a virgin . . . and not give the least jealousy even to his wife, the smallest grief to his children, or any scandal to the world.

His chief business in London, with his fellow members of the commission, was writing the permanent treaty of peace. It was a long and bitter contest. Great Britain had to be told to withdraw from American territory; she had some forts in the general area of the Great Lakes which, in fact, she did not abandon until years later. The United States demanded the return of the Negro slaves the British had seized and carried off when they were forced to retreat from various areas. There were the prewar debts of private American citizens to British traders, to be settled at a discount. The United States won two solid victories: the right to fish in Canadian waters, and to travel and trade on the Mississippi.

During his last year in London, Adams dashed off his book on what should be in the constitutions of the states; it was in three volumes, two of which appeared in 1787 and the third early in the following year. This *Defence of the Constitutions* was a sloppy job, written in great haste—so great that Adams, ordinarily punctilious, used substantial passages from other authors without credit. In spite of these defects, it had an immediate wide circulation in the United States, where the problem was now an urgent one. As I have said, it prevented some harebrained proposals by various wild men from being frozen into state constitutions, where they would have been hard to eradicate.

Arthur Lee called it "the work of the greatest genius that has ever written in this country."

Busy in one European capital after another, Adams missed the dismal period between the British surrender and the writing of the Constitution. When the text of this reached them in London, both he and Jefferson had grave misgivings about it. Like Franklin, they thought certain provisions were dangerous. Jefferson feared that the President might assume dictatorial powers, and Adams felt that the Senate, with two Senators from each state, had too much influence. Nevertheless they agreed with Franklin that this was probably as good a Constitution as could be adopted, and that some clear-cut form of federal organization was imperative.

Adams was now even more restive than before, and insisted on resigning and coming home. There was trouble about his departure; Congress forgot to tell England and the Netherlands that he was leaving, but he took the bit in his teeth and he and Abigail sailed in April 1788. Even before he got home, the people of Massachusetts had elected him to the first Congress organized under the new Constitution, but he declined to serve. Arriving in Boston in June, he took a badly needed long vacation for the remainder of the year. He had bought a new house in Braintree, now renamed Quincy, and he wanted plenty of time to get settled in it.

Early in 1789, the beloved Washington was made the first President. Adams was Vice-President, Jefferson Secretary of State, and Hamilton Secretary of the Treasury—the most distinguished quartet to serve simultaneously in these high offices in our history. Washington was chosen virtually by acclamation, but Adams did not do as well. The battle over the new Constitution had resulted in creating America's first two political parties; those who favored the Constitution became Federalists, and those who were against it, or wanted drastic modifications, were the Republicans, spiritual ancestors of the Democratic Party of today. Although Adams and Hamilton were both Federalists, they differed on many points, and Hamilton, who himself wanted to be Vice-President, managed to keep the vote for Adams from being unanimous, as it was for Washington; the Father of his Country got sixty-nine electoral votes, but Adams got only thirty-four. He was furious, and talked of refusing to serve, but finally accepted the position.

The next eight years as Vice-President were almost as frustrating as his tour of duty abroad. He was loyal to the President, but loyalty did not paralyze his judgment; he once told Gilbert Stuart that "Washington got the reputation of being a great man because he kept his mouth shut." Nobody could think of any job for the Vice-President (as was to be true for the next 170 years) except to preside over the Senate. Adams, who had firm opinions on every possible subject and was accustomed to express them freely on all occasions, found himself muzzled for the first time in his life, and hated it. Only very rarely was he called upon to break a tie with his vote, though on a few occasions his action was of great importance.

Again he had to be separated from his family much of the time, since Abigail had frequent duties in

Quincy. Writing to her in 1795 to complain of the dullness of life in Philadelphia, he remarked: "The old routine grows too insipid. I shall never be weary of my old wife, however; so declares Your affectionate husband." They had been married thirty-one years.

Washington's two terms were marked by serious conflicts with France and England. At about the time that Washington began to serve, the French Revolution broke out; nearly all America's old friends in Paris were swept out of office, and some of them were executed. The United States was divided in its sympathies; the Republicans like Jefferson favored the Revolution, which seemed to them to have similarities to their own; the Federalists, who tended to be conservative, were increasingly alarmed as the French working class and tenant farmers took more and more control.

The American Revolution had been, of course, no revolution at all, by modern standards, or even those of France in the 1790s. It did not seek to subvert the social order, or change the economic pattern; it represented only the desire of the colonists to govern themselves.

The new revolutionary leaders in Paris sent a Minister to America, Citizen Edmond Genêt, who began throwing his weight around the moment he landed. Some people, like Hamilton, feared to recognize him at all, lest this bring down on America the animosity of all the rest of Europe, strongly opposed to French efforts to "export their revolution." Genêt finally became so rash in his actions that a new man was sent to replace him, but in the meantime the

Americans had come almost to the brink of civil war over this issue.

The trouble with England was also dangerous. The British, unable to adjust to the fact that the United States was now an independent country, continued their bad habit of stopping American ships at sea and kidnapping sailors to serve in their navy. The United States lacked the ships and guns to protect her vessels and crews, though she soon started building a navy of her own. Despite her weakness, many people wanted to declare war on England, and several times the Senate was evenly divided on the question; Adams relieved the pressure by casting the deciding vote for peace.

The Spanish were another problem; the British had held Florida for twenty years, but it went back to Spain in 1783, with no boundary clearly defined, and the Spanish were claiming a huge territory. Not until 1819 did they reluctantly turn Florida over to the United States.

And finally, there were the Barbary pirates of North Africa, who demanded large bribes not to seize American ships and their cargoes and hold the sailors for ransom or sell them for slaves.

In 1792 Washington was again elected unanimously. Adams was reelected Vice-President, this time by 77 electoral votes out of 132. In 1794 it was felt that a new commercial treaty with England should be written, and John Jay was sent to London to do this. He had to make some humiliating concessions, but he did persuade England to abandon her forts in the Northwest Territory. The treaty was received in America with howls of rage from people who did not understand all the circumstances, but was finally ratified by a narrow margin.

In 1796 Washington refused a third term, setting a precedent that was not to be broken until 1940. In his famous farewell address he warned against a big public debt and a too large military establishment, stressed the need for the checks and balances of the Constitution, and emphasized the value of an enlightened public opinion. He also warned against favoritism toward any one foreign nation and against a permanent alliance with anybody. He left office (with three more years to live) on a strong tide of national affection.

It had long been evident that Adams would run for President, and that Jefferson would be his opponent; the Virginian had resigned as Secretary of State some time earlier, and Adams was convinced that he did so to clear the way for his candidacy. The campaign was savage, with wild charges on both sides. Adams was handicapped by the covert opposition of Hamilton, but he nevertheless won the election in December, with 71 out of 139 votes. Jefferson, as the second candidate, became Vice-President, under a system that was soon to be changed.

The bitter campaign left its scars on John. Describing his inauguration to Abigail, back in Quincy, he addressed her as "my dearest friend" and went on:

> Your dearest friend never had a more trying day than yesterday. A solemn scene it was indeed, and it was made more affecting to me

> by the presence of the General [Washington], whose countenance was as serene and unclouded as the day. He seemed to me to enjoy a triumph over me. Methought I heard him say, "Ay! I am fairly out and you fairly in! See which of us will be happiest."

Adams' four years in the Presidency were almost as frustrating as the previous eight years had been. The government had moved in 1790 from New York to Philadelphia, to wait a decade, as it turned out, until the new town of Washington could be erected on the swampy land along the Potomac. President Washington was slow in getting out of the Executive Mansion in Philadelphia, while the impatient Adams marked time; George owned all the furniture of the Mansion, and took it with him. The new President made a serious blunder by taking over Washington's Cabinet intact; several of its members were conspiring with Hamilton, and were ready to sabotage the new administration.

The trouble with France was growing steadily more serious. The French were capturing neutral ships carrying British cargoes, since the two nations were again at war, and Adams was forced to summon a special session of Congress to deal with the crisis. The hotheads wanted a declaration of war, but Adams refused.

Yet he was now more popular with the country than he had been before. His inaugural address had been very well received; his cousin, old Sam Adams, who had quarreled with him years earlier, was now reconciled and called him "the First Citizen of the United States—I may add, of the world." The change in attitude toward John is summed up by his biographer, Page Smith:

> [Affection for him began to be felt] not publicly or self-consciously, but through some kind of interior illumination. It showed itself in dozens of small ways; in spontaneous expressions of affection from the citizens of some distant rural community who suddenly felt a kind of comfort and assurance in that stout, indomitable little man who would do what he thought was right, regardless of party, press, the powers and potentates of the earth, or all the hounds of hell that might howl about him; it showed itself in comments from the leaders of the opposition party; in the abashed and awkward gestures of reconciliation from friends, who had distrusted his political principles. It was clear that whether he was a monarchist or not weighed little against his special virtues as Chief Executive of the United States.

Adams did not actually want a monarchy in the United States, though many people thought so. It is true, however, that like thousands of other Americans, he found it impossible suddenly to shake off the habits of thought of many years spent as an Englishman under the forms of English society. He flirted occasionally with the ideas of a President elected for life, of titles of nobility, and of ceremonial forms of address that were anathema to those Americans who admired the new order in France where everyone was "Citizen," just as everyone is "Comrade" in Russia today. As he made clear years later in his correspondence with Jefferson, he believed only in aristocracy based on personal merit, and recognized how rarely these virtues are transmitted intact to another generation.

As the tension with France steadily mounted, Congress passed the notorious Alien and Sedition Laws of 1798. Adams did not initiate these measures, but he approved of them, and signed them into law. The Sedition Act provided severe penalties for speaking or writing in criticism of the government or its officials. It was used against some Republican editors, and hung over the heads of many others as a threat. A temporary measure, it expired in two years.

The last years of Adams' Presidency were unhappy ones. French ships continued to prey on American vessels and there was a real, though undeclared, war between the two countries. In this crisis, Washington came back from retirement to be Commander in Chief of a new army which, on paper, consisted of ten thousand men. Keels were laid for some warships, to be built at a furious pace.

Paying taxes to the federal government was an idea so new that many people resented it strongly. When some of them were put into jail for refusal to pay, armed mobs broke down the doors and set them free.

Adams at last woke up to the fact that several members of the Cabinet were really Hamilton's men, and demanded some resignations. As a reprisal, Hamilton wrote a bitter attack on him, which was published in papers controlled by the opposing party, the Republicans, and caused a nationwide sensation.

John, who always wanted to be at his home in Massachusetts more than anywhere else in the world, spent what many people considered a scandalous proportion of his time there, instead of staying in the capital. One reason was that Abigail was seriously ill. He was also harassed by the problem of his son Charles, now a hopeless alcoholic, and soon to die of it. Charles had been given money by his brother, John Quincy, to invest, and had squandered it.

John gave John Quincy several diplomatic jobs to do; although these were well carried out, his enemies hurled the charge of nepotism at him. Matters were not helped by the fact that very late in his administration he nominated a son-in-law and a nephew to government posts.

Relations with France fluctuated with the comparative success or failure of that country's armies, now under the command of Napoleon Bonaparte. After the disastrous failure of their Egyptian campaign of 1798, the French were more amenable; Napoleon, who seized power a year later, calling himself First Consul, was a hard bargainer.

Adams ran again in the election of 1800, but it was obvious that his chances were not good. Hamilton was undercutting him in every possible way, his "appeasement" of France counted against him, and Jefferson and Aaron Burr, both of whom were in the race, made damaging charges. In the midst of all his other troubles, he had to move to Washington in September 1800 to occupy the almost completed

White House. Abigail was still in Quincy, too ill to travel, and on the evening of his first day in his new home he wrote her an often-quoted letter:

> Before I end my letter, I pray Heaven to bestow the best of blessings on this house and all that shall hereafter inhabit it. May none but wise and honest men ever rule under this roof.

When Abigail followed him to Washington a week later, she was disappointed with the raw, half-empty town, commenting that it had "houses scattered over a space of ten miles, and trees and stumps in plenty." The White House was so cold and drafty that she kept thirteen fires going.

When the election took place, Jefferson and Burr were tied with seventy-three votes each, and Adams had only sixty-five. Page Smith lists some of the reasons for his failure to win a second term as Washington had done, in addition to the unpopularity created by his keeping the peace with France. People feared a standing army, objected to taxes, were upset by Adams' quarrels with members of his Cabinet, and by now had come to see the harm done by the Alien and Sedition Acts. The opposing Republicans had great strength in some of the populous states like Pennsylvania. Voters found the Federalists dogmatic and inflexible. Above all, the division between the wings of that party weakened their cause. Yet even so, as Smith points out, the change of only a few hundred votes in New York State would have reelected Adams.

The outgoing President has been criticized because

he did not attend the inauguration of his successor; Smith thinks perhaps he had not been invited. Adams has been attacked even more sharply because on the night of his last day as President, he sat up very late appointing scores of federal judges, packing the bench with Federalists who thought as he did. He made one excellent nomination, of John Marshall to be Chief Justice of the Supreme Court, but many others were far less defensible.

The last quarter century of his life, spent in the Adams mansion in Quincy, surrounded by children and grandchildren, was in some ways the most peaceful of his entire stormy career. Butterfield Lyman says that "he retired to the house in Quincy he named 'Peacefield,' where he chewed the cud of frustration and relived his public life in long, self-justifying letters and memoirs," but his correspondence from this period reflects other moods as well.

When he left the Presidency he was badly worried about money, but his fears proved groundless. Abigail had managed to save some of the salary he received from his public offices, and had invested it sensibly. He still owned a big farm (by Massachusetts standards) which helped provide a living, in cash or farm products, and for some years he practiced a little law. The events of the great world seemed to ring only faintly in his ears; for example, in his correspondence with Jefferson there is little discussion of the War of 1812 with Great Britain.

The most important thing in Adams' last decade and a half was probably his reconciliation with Jefferson. They had been friends from the beginning of the Revolution until they served together in Washington's Presidency, when they moved apart for various reasons. It was their common friend, Dr. Benjamin Rush of Philadelphia, who succeeded in bringing them together, with tactful letters to both of them, to which each man responded by denying that they had ever quarreled. Adams now made the first overture, in 1812, and did it with an elaborate joke. On New Year's Day, he wrote from Quincy to Jefferson at Monticello saying, "As you are a friend to American manufacturers . . . I take the liberty of sending you by the post a packet containing two pieces of homespun lately produced in this quarter by one who was honored in his youth with some of your attention and much of your kindness." He then gave some news of his family, ending, "I wish you, Sir, many happy New Years . . . I am, Sir, with a long and sincere esteem, Your Friend and Servant."

The mail was slower in those days than now, and by January 21, the packet of "homespun" had not arrived. Jefferson did not wait for it, but wrote in a friendly way about the weaving done at Monticello. He reported that he rode horseback three or four hours a day, and made a round trip of 180 miles to a piece of land of his three or four times a year. He had heard that Adams walked a great deal but he himself was not now able to do so. He noted with sadness that only eight signers of the Declaration of Independence were still alive, of whom he was the only one in the South. He had given up reading newspapers in favor of Tacitus, Thucydides, Newton, and Euclid. He concluded in a friendly way, "No circumstances have lessened the interest I feel in these particulars [of Adams' health] respecting yourself; none have suspended for one moment my sincere esteem for you, and I now salute you with unchanged affection and respect."

When the "homespun" arrived, it proved to be two volumes of lectures that had been delivered by Adams' son, John Quincy. Both men now resumed writing to each other voluminously, and went on for more than a decade. Many of the letters have been lost, but we still have about fifty by Jefferson and twice as many by Adams, some of them three or four thousand words. Jefferson often delayed replying to his friend in Quincy until some time had elapsed; Adams, on the contrary, answered almost immediately. He once remarked, "Never mind if I write four letters to your one, your one is worth more than my four."

Old age mellowed Adams into paying compliments. He told Jefferson, "Your character in history may easily be foreseen. Your administration will be quoted by philosophers as a model of profound wisdom; by politicians as weak, superficial and short-sighted. Mine . . . will have no character at all."

The two old friends ranged over a multitude of themes. They agreed that the universe is endless and eternal. They discussed religion but got nowhere, though Adams remarked that "the Bible is the best book in the world." They both read Plato and disliked him heartily; Adams said, "My disappointment was very great, my astonishment was greater, and my disgust was shocking"; Jefferson thought the *Republic* was a work of "whimsies, puerilities and unintelligible jargon."

Adams was bitter about despotism, and felt that it could appear in a group as well as an individual. In words that seem to prophesy the policies of Soviet Russia in the twentieth century, he wrote:

> The fundamental article of my political creed is that despotism, or unlimited sovereignty or absolute power, is the same in a majority of a popular assembly, an aristocratical council, an oligarchical junto and a single emperor. Equally arbitrary, cruel, bloody, and in every respect diabolical. Accordingly, arbitrary power, wherever it has resided, has never failed to destroy all records, memorials, and histories of former times, which it did not like, and to corrupt and interpolate such as it was cunning enough to preserve or tolerate.

He still thought Jefferson was too soft on revolution, and attributed this to the fact that the Virginian had been President in a time of comparative calm. He recalled the terrorism that accompanied Shays' Rebellion in Massachusetts, and the time when, in 1793, ten thousand people milling in the streets of Philadelphia had threatened to kidnap President Washington to force him to help the French revolutionaries. He added that wise men had told him, "Nothing but the yellow fever . . . saved the United States from a total revolution." Even during his own administration he had been forced to have guns brought into his house by the back door to defend the lives of those within. (Not only were the friends of France bitter at this time, but there were mutinies in the army because Congress was badly in arrears as to their pay.) He thought there was less freedom for the individual than most people supposed.

> I cannot contemplate human affairs without laughing or crying. I choose to laugh. When people talk of the freedom of writing, speaking, or thinking, I cannot choose but laugh. No such thing ever existed. No such thing now exists; but I hope it will exist. But it must be hundreds of years after you and I shall write and speak no more.

Yet he admired the times in which he and Jefferson had accomplished their greatest work. The eighteenth century,

> notwithstanding all its errors and vices, has been, of all that are past, the most honorable to human nature. Knowledge and virtue were increased and diffused; arts, sciences, useful to men, ameliorating their condition, were improved more than in any former equal period.

It was Adams who raised philosophical questions, to which Jefferson sometimes replied, laconically. What good are pain and suffering, John wanted to know, and answered himself: Pleasure and pain cannot be separated; grief sobers you and makes you learn philosophy and resolve to be better. Would you live your life over if you had one million moments of pleasure and one million moments of pain? Adams said, no, he would not. Well, would you live your life over if you could have seventy-two years like the ones already past, but have one year of constant pain from things like gout and headache? Again he answered in the negative.

John took a very dim view of political parties:

> While all other sciences have advanced, that of government is still at a stand: little better understood, little better practiced now than three or four thousand years ago. What is the reason? I say, parties and factions will not suffer improvements to be made. As soon as one man hints at an improvement, his rival opposes it. No sooner has one party discovered or invented an amelioration of the condition of man or the order of society, than the opposite party belies it, misconstrues it, misrepresents it, ridicules it, insults it and persecutes it.

Though he was eight years older than his friend in Virginia he was in some ways more active. He reported that he had read forty-three volumes in one year, twelve of them quartos. Jefferson apologetically replied that he had read only half a dozen, and these of the smaller size, octavo. The friends from time to time gave or lent each other books; they were not drowning in a sea of print as we are today, and books were scarce and correspondingly cherished.

When Abigail died, on October 28, 1818, at

seventy-four, Jefferson wrote a letter of consolation, to which Adams replied:

> Your letter of November 13 gave great delight, not only by the divine consolation it afforded me under my great affliction, but as it gave me full proof of your restoration to health.
>
> While you live, I seem to have a bank at Monticello, on which I can draw for a letter of friendship and entertainment when I please.

By the 1820s, Adams' health was frail indeed. His palsy was so bad that for a time he had to hold the pen in both hands, and finally, took to dictating to one of his grandchildren. Since he was no longer able to undertake his famous long walks, his grandson built him a rather rigid carriage, whose jolting nearly killed him, but he refused to reveal this fact to the boy.

Lafayette, now himself a very old man, returned to the United States for a triumphal tour, and visited Adams at Quincy. There is a story, which sounds as though it must be apocryphal, that Adams afterward said, "That was not the Lafayette I knew," while Lafayette commented, "That was not the John Adams I knew."

Yet John still turned an undaunted face to the world.

> I am not tormented [he wrote] with the fear of death; nor, though suffering under many infirmities and agitated by many afflictions, weary of life . . . We shall leave the world with

> many consolations; it is better than we found it—superstition, persecution and bigotry are somewhat abated, governments are a little ameliorated, science and literature are greatly improved and more widely spread. Our country has brilliant and exhilarating prospects before it.

In the winter of 1825 the famous painter, Gilbert Stuart, himself now seventy, came to Quincy and made a new portrait of Adams, whom he had painted many years before. John was asked whether he would take part in the fiftieth anniversary of the signing of the Declaration, on July 4, 1826. He replied that he could not, because of his frail health, but he sent an optimistic message, predicting "a better condition of the human race." When the day came he was in a coma, with his family and closest friends at his bedside. He roused himself enough to utter his last three words, "Thomas Jefferson survives." But it was not true; Jefferson had died a few hours earlier.

Adams is one of the Presidents whose reputation has grown with the passage of years. His biographer, Page Smith, sums up the achievements of his four years in office. In 1797, the country was terribly torn by bitter factional disputes, and only the great prestige of George Washington held it together. By his stubbornness, Adams managed to avoid war with England or France, which might have been fatal, and he restored some unity. When he left office in 1801, the country had at least the beginning of a small army and navy, and the treasury was solvent—enormous achievements considering the difficulties with which he had to cope.

President John F. Kennedy, reviewing the new edition of Adams' *Diary and Autobiography* in *The American Historical Review* for January 1963, said that "to trace his relentless mastery of many different strands of law is awesome" and spoke of "his generous hospitality to new experience and ideas, a sharp eye for detail and color, [and] considerable anecdotal leaven . . . Adams conveys honesty, tenacity and pungent good sense." And in another place, Kennedy noted that "his spirit was the spirit of personal independence this country has always needed and encouraged . . . John Adams, in his bold and eloquent defense of unpopular justice, demonstrated the courage and conscience that has made this country great."

three

Thomas Jefferson: The All-Purpose Man

BY COMMON consent of all Americans, Jefferson is one of the three greatest men of our past, with Washington and Lincoln. It was Lincoln himself who said of him, "the principles of Jefferson are the definition and axioms of free society," and called him "the man who, in the concerted pressure of a struggle for national independence by a single people, had the coolness, foresight, and capacity to introduce into a merely revolutionary document an abstract truth, applicable to all men and all times, and so to embalm it there that today and in all coming days it shall be a rebuke and a stumbling block to the very harbingers of reappearing tyranny and oppression."

Jefferson was the universal man, as amazing as Leonardo da Vinci in the breadth of his interests and abilities. He wrote the Declaration of Independence and by it helped shape the character of the Revolution, and the nation that emerged. His was the chief role in setting up the decimal system for our currency. He was the father of the free, universal public school. By his Louisiana Purchase, which stretched his legal authority to the limit, he doubled the size of the United States at a cost of about four cents an acre.

He abolished entail and primogeniture, the system under which landed estates cannot be sold or divided but must descend intact to the eldest son—a system incompatible with a truly democratic republic. He helped to end, first in Virginia and then everywhere, the tax-supported state Church, and thus made possible true freedom of religion.

Jefferson was abroad when the American Constitution was written, but on his return home, it was he who insisted upon the all-important amendments, the Bill of Rights, safeguarding freedom of religion, of speech, of the press, guaranteeing trial by jury, forbidding excessive bail and cruel and unusual punishment, and reserving to the states all rights not specifically delegated to the federal government.

It was Jefferson who insured the victory of the

North in the Civil War, and thus preserved the Union. He had insisted that the vast Northwest Territory should come into the United States as free territory, and thus guaranteed that the states made out of it would be on the antislavery side.

His Lewis and Clark Expedition opened men's eyes to the vastness of the continent and its potential riches. Our first great secular institution of higher learning, the University of Virginia, was almost solely his achievement. He was an expert in agriculture, archaeology, architecture, and profoundly learned in philosophy, medicine, and philology. He practiced crop rotation, soil conservation, and contour plowing a century before these became standard practice, and invented a plow superior to any other then in existence. His book *Notes on the State of Virginia* was the first scientific work based on factual observation ever produced in this country, and a landmark in the history of science, coming at a time when most writers preferred to explore their own souls rather than the world around them. He had a profound influence on architecture throughout America, especially when he discarded the Corinthian column in favor of the Ionic, believing that the latter would be easier for American craftsmen to execute. Many of his ingenious gadgets are still remembered—his machine for copying documents, his outdoor-indoor weathervane, his rotating desk, his one-way staircases between kitchen and dining room.

He collected not one but two of the greatest private libraries in the country, one of which became the foundation of the Library of Congress. When he was in his early thirties a contemporary wrote of him that he could "plot an eclipse, survey a field, plan an edifice, break a horse, play the violin and dance the minuet." It is not surprising that President Kennedy, giving a dinner party for leaders in the arts and sciences, including a number of winners of the Nobel Prize, remarked, "I think this is the most extraordinary collection of talent, of human knowledge, that has ever been gathered together at the White House—with the possible exception of when Thomas Jefferson dined alone."

Jefferson was born in 1743. His father was a prosperous, self-educated man, a public surveyor, and a colonel in the militia. His mother was a member of an old and famous Virginia family, the Randolphs. The death of his father left him, at fourteen, with the responsibilities only the oldest male could, in those days, assume. He spent two years at William and Mary College, where he was profoundly influenced by a great teacher of mathematics, Dr. William Small, who started him on his lifelong interest in many branches of science. For a few years he practiced law, but soon abandoned this career to serve his country, in the Virginia Legislature, as Governor of that state, in Congress, as Ambassador to France, Secretary of State, Vice-President, and President for two terms.

How times have changed in America may be seen when we consider the State Department when Jefferson became Secretary under President Washington. He reported to his family that his duties were these: He must (1) take the census, (2) have charge of patents and copyrights, (3) control all federal marshals and attorneys, (4) see to the publication of all laws and distribute them to state governments, (5) correspond with the federal judges, (6) manage the mint, (7) conduct all correspondence with American ambassadors abroad, and (8) take care of the Great Seal. The entire State Department, aside from himself, consisted of only five people: a chief clerk and two assistants, a doorkeeper, and a messenger boy. I fear, he wrote home to his family, that I shall have little leisure.

In 1800, Jefferson ran for President. In those days, as noted, the man who received the largest vote in the Electoral College became President, and the next man became Vice-President, even though he might be entirely out of sympathy with the views of the Chief Executive. Aaron Burr, far inferior to Jefferson in most ways, was by now powerful in New York State politics, and both men received the same number of votes, thus throwing the election into the House of Representatives. The conservative, aristocratic Federalists came to Jefferson with an offer: If he would agree to support certain specified proposals of theirs, they would insure his election. The temptation must have been great, but Jefferson instantly refused. After thirty-six ballots, he won anyhow, largely because the Federalist leader, Alexander Hamilton, decided he was the lesser of two evils.

Jefferson's democratic simplicity is illustrated by the famous story of his first inauguration as President. When John Adams, his predecessor, was inaugurated he arrived at the scene in an elaborate state coach, surrounded by an entourage of many persons; Jefferson is said to have arrived all alone on horseback, modestly attired, tied his horse to a fence, and strolled over to be sworn in.

On New Year's Day, 1802, there was heavy snow in the new national capital, Washington, when a big country sleigh drew up before the White House. On it was a mammoth cheese, weighing more than twelve hundred pounds. The two men on the sleigh dismounted, but before they could reach the front door, President Jefferson was out on the steps, smiling and shaking hands.

John Leland and Darius Brown explained their errand. They had come, taking three weeks on the road, from the little town of Cheshire in western Massachusetts, where the citizens were warm admirers of the President. Since the town was named for the British county famous for its cheeses, they decided to make a big one for the President, and this they had done. After they had explained their mission, John Leland, who was a minister, read a statement avowing the loyalty of the citizens of Cheshire to the Constitution, and offered a prayer thanking "that supreme Father of the universe, who . . . has raised up a Jefferson for this critical day, to defend republicanism and baffle all the arts of aristocracy."

The President had the cheese put in the East Room of the White House which he renamed in its honor the Mammoth Room. The name tickled everyone; Jefferson was famous for his interest in the bones of the prehistoric mastodon, and his political enemies had taken to calling him Mr. Mammoth. Later, at the annual New Year's Day reception, everyone was invited to taste the cheese—after the President had cut out a big wedge to go back to the town of Cheshire. While the scarlet-coated Marine Band played martial airs, Cabinet officers and their wives, ambassadors, other dignitaries, blanketed chiefs of the Miami and Potawatomi tribes, and practically everybody else in Washington, tasted the cheese and pronounced it excellent.

The parson and Darius stayed on a few days as Jefferson's guests; before they departed he persuaded them to accept some money from his slender private purse to be spent on any public project the citizens of Cheshire might select. The sum was more than the value of the cheese; the President took care never to accept gifts while in office.

The incident is illustrative of Jefferson's character in more ways than one. It reveals his simplicity, his tact in dealing with plain citizens, the sense of humor that made him turn a joke against himself, and his scrupulous respect for the office he held.

This great democrat objected to the use of titles like "Your Excellency" or "the Honorable"; he wanted to be called "Mr. Jefferson," and he got his way. He refused to have a big ball in celebration of his birthday. Once a foreign ambassador called on him in full-dress uniform, with a ceremonial sword; Jefferson received him in casual dress, wearing slippers.

Jefferson was six feet two, thin and erect, with a ruddy complexion and angular features. As a young man his hair was red, but in middle life it was sandy in color; his eyes were gray, flecked with hazel. He enjoyed robust health which he attributed chiefly to abstemiousness with food and drink, and to taking outdoor exercise every day; in Paris, he walked five or six miles daily through the streets, and at Monticello he spent several hours in the saddle.

Jefferson married early and had six children, only two of whom lived to maturity. His wife, Martha, to whom he was deeply devoted, died after ten years of married life; Jefferson in his grief shut himself up in his study for three weeks, pacing the floor night and day until completely exhausted.

He was strongly attracted to at least one other woman; when he was in France he became a close friend of Mrs. Maria Cosway, a painter and the wife of a popular English painter of miniatures. Whether she was really fond of Jefferson, or merely used her friendship with him to advance her husband's career, is not clear. The relationship was soon broken off, after it had produced a famous letter by Jefferson to her, the longest he ever wrote, in which "the head and the heart" argued, and the head won—but just barely. A minor result of the Cosway episode was that, out walking with her one day he tried to vault a fence and broke his right wrist so badly that it troubled him for the rest of his life; he was forced to learn to write with his left hand.

Like almost every great man, he lived a life of tremendous mental and physical activity. Even in his seventies he got up at dawn, remarking once, "the sun has not caught me in bed for fifty years." He wrote and read until his early breakfast, then he read for another half hour, and divided the rest of the morning among the garden, his workshops, and his library. From one to three he was on horseback, then had his chief meal of the day, and relaxed with his family and friends until he went to bed about 10 P.M. He read the classics in Latin and Greek, and modern books in French, Spanish and Italian. He also knew some Anglo-Saxon.

For many years the nation was rocked by the bitter ideological quarrel between Hamilton, aristocratic, conservative, a believer in control by a power elite, and Jefferson, the democrat, friend of the farmer and the working man, who trusted the instincts of the common people over the arrogance of the rich. Some of his best friends broke with him on this issue, and he was saddened when he would see one of them cross the street to avoid meeting him.

He himself shared no such sentiment. He knew that honest men can differ honestly, and never willingly permitted a friendship to be impaired for such a cause. "They must love misery indeed," he wrote sadly, "who would rather at the sight of an honest man feel the torment of hatred and aversion rather than the benign spasms of benevolence and esteem."

As the years went by, some of these former friends became reconciled, chief among them John Adams. As I have recorded, for the last decade and more of the lives of these two men, they were in constant correspondence between Monticello and Quincy, Massachusetts, and their letters are one of the glories of American historical literature.

Repeatedly during his life, Jefferson gave proof of his personal courage. He was one of the first men in the United States brave enough to be actually vaccinated against smallpox, at a time when to do so was considered very risky.

The terrible yellow-fever epidemic in Philadelphia took place when that city was still the capital of the United States, and long before the cause of the disease was known. Nearly everyone who could do so fled from the city; Jefferson noted with amusement that his archenemy, Alexander Hamilton, was among those who ran away. He himself stayed in town until his duties were fully completed, and then, unhurried, set out for his beloved Monticello.

Through the darkest days of the Revolution, Jefferson refused to give way to despair or defeatism. All his life when skies were dark, he looked forward to a sunnier tomorrow. "How much pain," he remarked, "have cost us the evils which have never happened! My temperament is sanguine. I steer my barque with hope in the head [the prow], leaving fear astern." His whole philosophy made him repudiate strongly the idea of accepting other people's opinions ready made. He believed every man should form his own ideas on every subject. "Neither believe nor reject anything," he wrote to his nephew, Peter Carr, "because any other person or descriptions [classes] of persons have rejected or believed it. Your own reason is the only oracle given you by heaven, and you are answerable, not for the rightness, but the uprightness of the decision."

Very early in life, he attained a prominent place among the leaders, first of Virginia and then of the country. This was primarily because of his skill as a writer; his colleagues quickly learned that he could draft a document better than anyone else. When the time came to write the Declaration of Independence, a committee was appointed of which he was a member, but the actual draftmanship was his. Many millions of people all over the world have thrilled to his flaming words: "We hold these truths to be self-evident, that all men are created equal, that they are endowed by their Creator with certain unalienable rights, that among these are life, liberty, and the pursuit of happiness. That to secure these rights, governments are instituted among men, deriving their just powers from the consent of the governed . . . And for the support of this Declaration, with a firm reliance on the protection of Divine Providence, we mutually pledge to each other our lives, our fortunes, and our sacred honor."

Most of the Declaration is a detailed description of the grievances the American colonies had against the Crown. It was, partly, a piece of propaganda, the greatest and most effective in our history. Jefferson wrote it knowing that many Americans were not sure that the ties to the mother country should be broken; he wanted to persuade them. He also knew that the document would be circulated throughout Europe, and wished to make the position of the colonists clear.

Ben Franklin, the best other writer among the Revolutionary leaders, made a few changes of words, as I have recorded. The Congress also altered the original text slightly. The members took out his attack on the slave trade, in deference to the feeling of the Southern states. They also removed criticism of the British people, hoping to drive a wedge between them and the Crown. But these changes do not alter the fact that the Declaration is Jefferson's, a reflection of his mind and heart.

At one point during the Revolution, Jefferson feared that his public career was about to end in disgrace. The British made a series of surprise sorties through Virginia, which was almost undefended, and they came close to capturing Jefferson, then the Governor of that state, who was at Monticello, which is in rather rugged country. Hastily he put his family into a wagon, and sent them off with a trusted driver to safety. After a few imperative tasks, he mounted a horse, but perceived that by now the Redcoats were on the escape road. At top speed he rode up a nearby mountainside until at a safe distance, he stopped, hidden by trees, and looked down upon the soldiers overrunning his home. Then by a circuitous route he made his own escape.

He feared his career might be over, that he would never be forgiven by his countrymen for his retreat, even though it would have been folly to wait and be captured. But his pessimism was ill-founded. Although his enemies attacked him for "running away," he went on to his further great services.

Soon after the writing of the Declaration of Independence, Jefferson was called to Virginia to write a new state constitution, and a new draft of her legal code. Some of his views were too liberal for his colleagues at that time, but most of them were adopted during the next few years. In 1779, he was the obvious choice to be Governor of the state and he was reelected a year later. When Cornwallis surrendered at Yorktown, Jefferson became chairman of the committee charged with the difficult task of the peace negotiations.

Another famous document that came from his pen was the resolution adopted by Kentucky in 1798. This for the first time set forth clearly the doctrine of states' rights—that the federal government has no powers except those specifically delegated by the states, and that these should alone decide on the extent of those powers. Jefferson's work in this field had a tremendous effect on the history of the country—an effect still being felt.

He was an indefatigable writer. His complete works, now in the process of being published for the first time, will fill more than fifty volumes. He wrote at least fifty thousand letters, perhaps seventy-five thousand. The correspondence between him and John Adams by itself makes a good-sized book.

He also kept for years a "literary commonplace book" into which he copied favorite quotations from the volumes he was incessantly reading. Not only did he have these passages always available for easy reference, but the physical act of copying them printed them strongly in his memory.

As the first and greatest American publicist, Jefferson considered a free and widely circulated press to be all important. "The basis of our government," he wrote, "being the opinion of the people, the very first object should be to that right; and were it left to me to decide whether we should have a government without newspapers, or newspapers without a government, I should not hesitate a moment to prefer the latter."

This was, I believe, a bit of hyperbole; Jefferson knew he would never be confronted by such a choice, and so he felt free to use the shock value of his statement. But in the 1970s, when the role of the media of communication in relation to an enormously swollen and enormously powerful federal government is being challenged as never before, what he said is worth pondering. All over the world there is an increasing tendency for governments to hide the truth from the people; we might well remember Jefferson's strong opposition to all kinds of censorship. "It is error alone," he observed, "which needs the support of government. Truth can stand by itself. Subject opinion to coercion: Whom will you make your inquisitors? Fallible men; men governed by bad passions, by private as well as public reasons." He felt that the people "may safely be trusted to hear everything, true and false, and to form a correct judgment between them."

In 1814, he spoke out in defense of a Philadelphia bookseller arrested for selling a scientific book which the local authorities considered irreligious. Said Jefferson: "If [this] book be false in its facts, disprove them; if false in its reasoning, refute it. But for God's sake, let us freely hear both sides if we choose."

He lived up to his principles under the deepest stress. No American President was more cruelly vilified by the newspapers than he, yet he insisted they must suffer no government interference. "Our first object," he said to those who wished him to act, "should be to leave open all the avenues of truth. The most effectual (thus far) is the freedom of the press."

When the Federalist newspapers were abusing him he remarked that "they are like the chimneys to our dwellings; they carry off the smoke of party which might otherwise stifle the nation."

Politics in Jefferson's day was far more bitter than today; public men were attacked with accusations and with vituperative language that would be unthinkable now. Though Jefferson was for many years the object of terrible abuse, he made a lifelong policy of never responding. He summed up his philosophy in a letter to his friend, George Rogers Clark, the great explorer, who was also being viciously slandered: "That you have enemies, you must not doubt when you reflect that you have made yourself eminent. If you meant to escape malice you should have confined yourself within the sleepy line of regular duty."

Clark's antagonists would continue to hate him, Jefferson said, "if you continue to do good to your country and honor to yourself." And he observed to his friend, John Adams: "Men of energy of character must have enemies. There are two sides to every question. If you take one with decision and act on it with effect, those who take the other will of course be hostile in proportion as they feel that effect."

Jefferson was struck by the fact that the white Americans considered the Indians to be degenerate human beings, while many Europeans held the same view of the Americans. He disagreed with the first view as strongly as with the second. People should be judged, he felt, in the light of their own institutions, and not by standards alien to them. The Indians, he pointed out, had no government and no laws, in the

European sense; yet they were happier than the Europeans. They lived by their own public opinion, their own moral code, which worked far better than the system of punishments the Europeans had set up. He believed profoundly in guidance by an inward light. "A sense of right and wrong," he wrote to his nephew, Peter Carr, "is as much a part of man's nature as the sense of hearing, seeing and feeling."

This did not mean of course that instruction is not necessary. When his younger daughter, Maria, was to arrive in Paris, he told his older daughter, Martha, that she must take care of her sister. "Teach her to be always true; no vice is so mean as the want of truth, and at the same time so useless . . . Teach her never to be angry; anger only serves to torment ourselves, to divert others, and alienate their esteem." (Martha at the time was fifteen!)

He delighted in giving advice to this daughter. On another occasion he wrote reminding her that "nothing contributes more to your future happiness (moral rectitude always excepted), than contracting a habit of industry and activity. Of all the cankers of human happiness, none corrodes with so silent, yet so baneful a tooth as indolence . . . Exercise and application produce order in our affairs, health of body, cheerfulness of mind, and these make us precious to our friends."

Jefferson, like all of us, was sometimes disappointed by the actions of his friends, who failed to live up to his standards or their own, but he refused to descend into cynicism, and continued to accept every man as an honorable gentleman until he proved himself otherwise. "I cannot act," he said, "as if all men were unfaithful because some are so. I would rather be the victim of occasional infidelities than relinquish my general confidence in the honesty of men."

In his day, most philosophers thought that mankind is fundamentally evil and must be forced into good behavior by law and by the fear of eternal damnation. Jefferson repudiated this idea. "Nature has implanted in our breasts," he wrote, "a love of others, a sense of duty to them, a moral instinct." He believed that to create a healthy and successful society we need only to liberate this instinct.

This great man was also a warm and generous person; many a stranger who met him remarked that after a few minutes he felt as though they were old friends. All his life he went to tremendous pains to help those with whom he came into contact, most of whom had no claim on him. When he was seventy-seven he observed that in the course of the previous year he had written twelve hundred letters, nearly all of them to strangers requesting information, some of them thousands of words long.

On one occasion, a solitary traveler was making his way on foot through deep woods near the raw, new little town of Washington, D.C., and presently came to a stream where there was a ford but no bridge. Reluctant to get his clothes wet, he stood on the bank deliberating, until a band of horsemen approached, going in his direction. He waited until the last had reached him, and then asked whether he could mount behind the rider and cross the stream. Smiling, the equestrian complied. When they reached the other side, another of the horsemen, who had wheeled and waited for them, asked the traveler why he had chosen the last man in the group. He replied that the others had such forbidding countenances that he feared a refusal. But "the old gentleman looked as if he would do it, and so I asked him."

Did he know who it was? No, he didn't. "That was the President of the United States."

How far he was ahead of most people of his time is shown by his treatment of some Hessians in the British army who had been captured at Saratoga, and had been sent to Virginia, near Charlottesville, then believed to be far behind the lines. Most people heaped abuse on the captives, but not Jefferson. A general was among the captives; and in the easygoing habit of the times, he had his family with him. His daughter was the same age as Jefferson's, and they became friends. One of the aides played musical instruments, and helped Jefferson practice his rusty French.

When the British army got dangerously close, and it was planned to send the prisoners farther inland, Jefferson protested to the Governor. He pointed out that the captives had spent much of their own money repairing houses, buying seeds, and laying out gardens and even fields of grain with which they were feeding themselves, thus relieving the Treasury of some of its burden. In fact, he hoped that after the war, the Hessians would stay where they were, and become a permanent part of the community.

In 1786, Jefferson's diplomatic duties took him to

London, to the Court of the British King. When he was presented, George III gave him a cold, hard stare, with his piglike little eyes, and then turned his back and walked to the other end of the room. Jefferson was unruffled; he knew that the King had identified him as author of the Declaration of Independence, which had excoriated George in measured but deadly, unprecedented terms, and had played a great part in wresting from the monarch his most precious overseas colonies.

Jefferson was struck by the fact that no one ever invents anything all alone, that, as Newton said of himself, we "stand on the shoulders of giants." He himself drew his ideas from the books of ancient and modern philosophers which he read and reread; the Declaration of Independence, for example, owes much to John Locke.

Jefferson believed profoundly in personal investigation of anything that interested him. While still a young man, he was appointed to a committee to find out whether the South Branch of the James River was navigable by large boats; while the other members sat in the state capital and studied documents, Jefferson jumped into a canoe and paddled the length of the stream. He was greatly interested in the bones of prehistoric animals which were being unearthed in various parts of Virginia; whenever he heard of such a find, he got on his horse (roads suitable for carriages were few, and impassable in bad weather) and went to see.

When he was in France he seized every opportunity to explore the countryside and to talk with the peasantry and town working people. He sensed the rising discontent that was to bring on the French Revolution, before anybody in the Court, and pleaded with his old friend Lafayette to find out, as he himself was doing, what was going on.

In a day when most aristocrats would not deign to speak to those of humble origin, except to give an order, Jefferson was almost unique in going out of his way to talk to gardeners, maidservants, waiters, poor travelers on foot, whom he would take into his carriage for conversation when he overtook them on the road. He much preferred solid conversation with a gardener to the idle chatter of the French Court, to which he was frequently subjected. As he wrote, "From men of that class I have derived the most satisfactory information . . . and have sought their acquaintance with as much industry as I have avoided that of others who would have made me waste my time in good society."

For a gentleman to put the lowly at their ease so that they would speak freely was a real art in Jefferson's day. As he said to Lafayette, "You must be absolutely incognito. You must ferret the people out of their hovels as I have done, look into their kettles, eat their bread, loll on their beds in the pretense of resting yourself, but in fact to find if they are soft." If the Marquis would only do this, Jefferson told him, he could then "apply your knowledge to the softening of their beds or the throwing a morsel of meat into their kettle of vegetables." (Lafayette never did.)

Wherever Jefferson went, in any European country, he studied the trees and growing crops to see whether there was anything that America ought to have; he sent across the ocean a constant stream of seeds or small specimens for replanting.

On one occasion, a clergyman stopped at a Virginia tavern, and entering the common room, found there a modestly dressed, affable-seeming stranger. They entered into conversation about a public-works project in the neighborhood, and the clergyman realized the stranger must be a distinguished engineer. The talk turned to agriculture, and he saw he had been mistaken, that this man was the owner of great plantations. They spoke of religion, and he decided that his companion was a minister, though he could not be sure of the denomination. As soon as possible, he hurried to the innkeeper to find out the identity of this well-informed man, and was astonished to discover that this was the President.

At a time when nearly every public man in America condoned Negro slavery, Jefferson set his face against it. He tried unsuccessfully to have it repudiated by the state of Virginia and by Congress. He worked for the proposal that freed slaves should be set up in a country of their own, which was done years later when Liberia, in Africa, was established. He would presumably have freed his own slaves, most of whom he had inherited, if this had been possible, but it was not. During most of his life he had creditors who could have prevented this action as giving away property on which they had a lien. Moreover, there was no place in the South where freed slaves could live in security and make a decent life for themselves. He did free a few, when he thought it was safe to do so, and he let several others, so light in color that they could "pass" easily, slip away.

How well Jefferson treated his workers, both slaves and freemen, is shown by the reception he got when he returned to Monticello in 1789 after his years in France. When word came that he was soon to arrive, they asked for and received a holiday so that they could welcome him. It is reported that when his carriage neared the house, they unhitched the horses and, "with cries of delight," pulled the carriage up the last ridge of the mountain. Then they carried him to the house on their shoulders, laughing and crying, while those on the outskirts of the crowd sought to get near enough to touch his hand.

All his life Jefferson was an omnivorous reader. By the time he was seventy he had accumulated six thousand books, every one of which he had read, some of them repeatedly. When the British burned Washington in 1814, they destroyed the Library of Congress, which then consisted of three thousand works. As I have noted, Jefferson immediately offered his own library in its place, to be purchased at any price Congress wanted to pay, and this was done; today the Library of Congress, in its rare-book room, still has two thousand of Jefferson's original books.

The old man promptly began a new library at Monticello, and in the twelve years that remained to him, he built it up to about one thousand volumes, an amazing record in view of the scarcity of books and their high price.

It is more remarkable when we remember that Jefferson was hard-pressed for money in his old age.

He had inherited no private fortune, Monticello did not earn much, and his lifelong habit of pressing his hospitality on everyone who came his way, friend or stranger, was expensive. He endorsed a note for $20,000 for a friend who defaulted; Jefferson had to pay interest on the loan, and this took more than he could spare. Near the end of his life, he proposed to sell his estate through a lottery, but instead, the American people contributed to a fund to help him out. He died believing that Monticello was now safe, but this was not true; after his death his home, his library, and all his material possessions had to be sold.

Cruelest of all the attacks on him was one made by an unsavory character, editor of a Richmond, Virginia, newspaper, who published the charge that Jefferson had had a Negro mistress, and had had several children by her.

An enormous amount of keyhole journalism has grown up about this charge. The Negro slave in question was Sally Hemings, and she did in fact have seven children out of wedlock. Her mother was Elizabeth Hemings, who was the mistress of Jefferson's father-in-law, John Wayles. She in turn had been the result of a liaison between a British sea captain and an African woman; she was therefore half white, and her daughter had only one-quarter Negro blood.

Jefferson went to Paris as American Minister in 1785. In 1787, he sent for his eight-year-old daughter Maria (Polly), alarmed because his much younger daughter, Lucy, had just died of whooping cough. He asked that she be accompanied by a responsible, middle-aged woman slave, but for some inexplicable reason, she was sent instead with Sally, who had come with her mother and five brothers and sisters to live at Monticello when Mr. Wayles died. Sally was fourteen, only a child herself. She stayed in Paris with Jefferson until he returned to America in 1789. The scandalous story says that he began a liaison with Sally in Paris and continued it after he returned to Monticello. At least one of Sally's seven children boasted in later years that he was Jefferson's son, and the story was handed down for generations.

Illegitimate relations between Negro women slaves and their white masters were of course a commonplace in the South for many years before and after Jefferson. A Negro woman slave had no rights and was totally in the power of her white master; the Census of 1860, the last before the Civil War, listed 500,000 mulattos in the South, at a time when there were only 175,000 plantations. But the code of a gentleman (which most of the Southern slave owners insisted that they were) forbade him ever to admit fathering such offspring.

The "evidence" against Jefferson which busy modern scholars have dug up is circumstantial indeed. He is supposed to have taken especial care of Sally, though he never set her free; his daughter did so in 1828, two years after Jefferson's death.

The defenders of Jefferson say that two of his nephews, Peter and Samuel Carr, were the fathers of at least some of Sally's seven children.

Jefferson, under great pressure for many years to defend himself, steadfastly refused to do so. If he had told the facts, he would have had to reveal that the children of his father-in-law's liaison, including Sally, were the half-brothers and half-sisters of his own beloved wife.

Jefferson was famous for his generosity; the workers on his plantation did their best to keep him from giving away everything in sight. In 1816 there was a bad frost and all the corn in that part of Virginia was destroyed. Jefferson sent his overseer to a distant place where the corn had escaped the freeze, and bought thirty barrels at $10 a barrel. When it reached Monticello he began giving it away to poor farmers of the neighborhood until there was hardly any left. When his overseer protested, Jefferson said: "What can I do? These people tell me they have no corn and it will not do to let them suffer." The overseer, who knew which among his neighbors really needed help, finally persuaded Jefferson to permit a preliminary screening.

While he had difficulty with his personal finances as President, he managed those of the country very well. His administration was so economical that the public debt was reduced and the Treasury had a big surplus. Because of this he was able to abolish all internal taxes; in his second Inaugural Address he could boast, "What farmer, what mechanic, what laborer, ever sees a tax gatherer of the United States?" Times have changed.

Jefferson was unjustly accused of being an agnostic or atheist, though he repeatedly affirmed his belief in God. This was because of a single sentence of his, torn from its context and widely quoted, "It does me no injury for my neighbor to say there are twenty gods or no God. It neither picks my pocket nor breaks my leg." Jefferson had chosen this unfortunate illustration while intent on an argument that government should not interfere with a man's private beliefs that do no harm to others. The phrase was picked up and endlessly circulated by his enemies.

Among these were the clergy of the Established Church in Virginia, whose perquisites he had succeeded in reducing, who were correspondingly bitter against him. His opposition to a state Church was not religious but political. So strong was the feeling among the clergy that one minister refused to baptize a baby on learning that it had been named for Jefferson.

On many occasions he avowed his belief in a Supreme Being. He copied out all the words of Jesus from the New Testament, and circulated this "book" among his friends.

Jefferson was in France when the dreadful storm of the French Revolution was just about to break. One evening a group of important members of the governing regime asked him to confer with them about possible ways to avert the coming catastrophe. Though, strictly speaking, a foreign diplomat should have kept aloof from such matters, Jefferson readily agreed. He made a number of proposals for concessions by the King, which, if they had been carried out, might have averted one of the bloodiest revolutions of all time.

When he returned to his lodgings that night, Jefferson sat down, and following a lifelong habit, wrote out a summary of the conversation. He knew from his earliest years that the best way to clarify anything in your own mind is to make a written report of it; that most ideas hardly exist unless they can be put down.

During the early days of the American Revolution, he had followed this rule both in meetings of his fellow Virginians and those of the Continental Congress. Many important facts about the Revolution are known today only because of his memoranda.

A century before most philosophers had arrived at this view, Jefferson believed that constant change is not only inevitable, but should be welcomed and made to serve the purposes of mankind. "No society," he said, "can make a perpetual constitution, or even a perpetual law." He argued that it was immoral for the dead past to try to dictate to the present or the future. "The earth," he wrote to John Adams, "belongs to the living generation."

Conservatives (who wouldn't like him anyhow) have complained for many years about Jefferson's observation that "a little rebellion now and then is a good thing, and as necessary in the political world as storms are in the physical," and his parallel observation that "the tree of liberty must be refreshed from time to time with the blood of patriots and tyrants. It is their natural manure."

It seems unlikely that Jefferson held this view very seriously. The first quotation is from a private letter to James Madison, the second from one to William Stevens Smith, both written in the same year, 1787. As far as I know, he never expressed the same view again anywhere, and certainly not in any public statement.

But in any case, the sort of "rebellion" he had in

mind was very far from the ideological revolutions fomented by fascism and communism in the twentieth century. What he thought of was a rebellion against tyranny such as the British monarchy exercised against the American colonists, rebellion which, if successful, would continue the same sort of political and economic organization as before, as an independent entity. With his regard for the sacred rights of the individual, his deep love of freedom, we may be sure that if he were alive today he would be the bitterest foe of the totalitarian philosophy.

A few weeks before his death in 1826, the citizens of Washington invited him to come from Monticello to be guest of honor at the fiftieth anniversary of the signing of the Declaration of Independence. He, like John Adams, was obliged to reply that the state of his health would make this impossible. He took the occasion to make a stirring reaffirmation of his belief in democracy. "The mass of mankind," he wrote, "has not been born with saddles on their backs." His letter was immediately printed as a broadside and circulated through the United States.

On the very day of the celebration, July 4, 1826, he passed away. He had written his own epitaph: "Here was buried Thomas Jefferson, author of the Declaration of American Independence, of the Statute of Virginia for Religious Freedom, and father of the University of Virginia." (He did not bother to mention two terms as President!) Emblazoned on the beautiful Jefferson Memorial in Washington is another famous sentence of his: "I have sworn upon the altar of God eternal hostility against every form of tyranny over the mind of man." No American lived up to that pledge more truly than he.

four

Sojourner Truth: The Home-made Miracle

SHE WAS born the slave daughter of slave parents, probably in 1797, the year John Adams was settling into the Presidency. She died eighty-six years later, in the era of Chester A. Arthur, when she was the most famous woman of her race in the world, and one of the four or five best-known and best-loved women in America of any color. She worked heroically for many years throughout the North, often in grave personal danger, first for the abolition of slavery, and after that for many other causes, most notably for rights for women.

She never learned to read and write. For the first thirty years of her life she was a slave, and teaching a slave his letters was forbidden by law in most states, and by social custom in others. In her later years, when she was already famous, she was always traveling, enormously active, with little time to give to the classroom she had never entered in her life. There were invariably people eager to read to her what she needed, or to take her dictation. She had a wonderful memory; she composed many songs, words and music, and remembered them all. She could recite long passages from the Bible which was to her the revered Book of Books. She met and mingled with some of the great men and women of her day—Lincoln, Harriet Beecher Stowe, William Lloyd Garrison, Frederick Douglass, Susan B. Anthony, Wendell Phillips, Lucretia Mott, Lyman Beecher, Harriet Tubman. She talked with them, in public and private, on terms of perfect equality.

For decades, beginning in 1843, she traveled constantly on the roads of America, preaching the gospel of equality and justice. Her first and most important topic was freedom for her fellow Negroes, but she added to it freedom for women, and other causes. When she started, she went on foot, not knowing at the beginning of each day where she would lay her head that night. Later she used trains, often with a struggle to be allowed on board—a black woman; she was usually forced to sit in the smoking car, and finally began using a corncob pipe, preferring her own fumes to those of others. Sometimes she drove with a horse and buggy; since she could not read the roadside signs, she often said, "God, you drive," and let the reins loose. Wherever she went, she knew she would find people who welcomed her—as well as those bitterly antagonistic, who many times put her life in danger.

How much good did she do, with all those years of arduous, dangerous travel and speaking? No one can say; there is no computer for the effect of work like hers in her day. But she surely did as much as any other individual in her field, except perhaps Harriet Beecher Stowe, to help solidify Northern opinion against slavery, and to sow seeds for the emancipation of women which is beginning to be achieved more than a hundred years later. And she made many people, black and white, honor and love her.

Many of us tend to forget, conveniently, that slavery existed in the North as well as the South. In New York State, where she lived, it was abolished partly in 1817, but not completely until 1827. Most of the horrors of bondage in the South existed there, and had for two hundred years. Not only were there Negro slaves; in the early days there were white men and women as well, including some who were captured off sailing vessels by pirates and sold, as matter-of-factly as any transaction on the Barbary Coast. In New York City at the beginning of the nineteenth century there were hardly any schools a black child could attend; Negroes could ride only on those public vehicles marked "Colored permitted." Many professions and some trades were barred to them, by custom or in some places by law. (In the South, in the tense times of the 1850s, for a Negro to learn the printing trade could be punished by death.)

Nearly a hundred years after Sojourner was gone, many members of her race wished to be called *blacks*; but during her lifetime, that word, though it was used, had overtones of contempt. I prefer to employ in these pages chiefly the word she respected, and to which she gave honor.

Her presence was unmistakable in any crowd. She was six feet tall, erect, and carried herself with dignity. Her face was angular and usually sad; her gaze intelligent and keen. She always wore a long dress of gray or black, often with a white collar, and on her head a kerchief tied into a turban, or sometimes a white Quaker cap. Over it, especially when she was walking the roads in the burning sun, she had an ample sunbonnet. In cool weather she wore a shawl.

Her voice was deep and resonant, which helped spread the rumor, persisting for many years, that she was a man. Her speaking was enormously effective; she used humor, irony, indignation, strong emotion. Deeply religious, her speech was laced with references to the Deity; she believed she had had many Divine revelations. As she said, other people might talk with men, but she talked with God. Some of her sayings were quoted all over the country, and for many years.

One of her lifelong friends (though they differed on tactics) was Frederick Douglass. This brilliant and famous man was born into slavery in Maryland. His white owner's wife broke the law by teaching him to read when he was a child. As a young man he escaped to the North, and in 1845 published his autobiography. Since he was subject to seizure and return to slavery, he at once had to flee to England, where he lived for several years, until American friends bought his freedom. He came back and devoted the rest of his life to the Negro cause.

On one famous occasion, Douglass was speaking to a large audience, with Sojourner sitting quietly to one side. He was in a bitter mood of pessimism, and went on and on about the hopelessness of the situation of the slaves. Finally she stood up, and her great deep voice boomed across the room. "Frederick," she said, "is God dead?"

The crowd was thunderstruck, then burst into applause; she had turned its mood around. As Douglass said afterward, "We were all for a moment brought to a standstill, just as if someone had thrown a brick through the window." The phrase became so famous it is carved on Sojourner's tombstone in Battle Creek, Michigan.

As was to be expected in her circumstances, she did not use polished English. Her parents spoke only a bastard type of Dutch, and this was all she knew in her childhood. Her contemporaries, when they reported her speeches, put into her mouth the jargon then assumed to be a transliteration of Negro talk, especially that heard in the South which she never visited. Since they don't agree with each other, and bear no relation to any form of Negro speech known today, I have chosen to omit the attempts at dialect.

On one occasion she shared the platform with another speaker known to be an agnostic. During the meeting a bad lightning storm came up, and the thunder pealed over the building. A hysterical young man leapt to his feet, saying that God was about to destroy them all for listening to such a person. Sojourner looked at him calmly and said, "Child, don't be scared. You are not going to be harmed. I don't expect God has ever heard of you."

In her public appearances she was heckled by those in the audience who disagreed with her views on freedom for Negroes, for women, for everybody. One such heckler pointed out to her that "the United States Constitution has not a single word in it against slavery. Are you attacking the Constitution, old woman?"

This was a year when an infestation of weevils had destroyed many thousands of acres of wheat in the Middle West, a fact that gave Sojourner a topical theme for her reply. She said:

> This morning I was walking out, and I climbed over a fence. I saw the wheat holding up its head, looking so big. I went up and took hold of it. Would you believe it? There was no wheat there! I said, "God, what's the matter with this wheat?" And He said to me, "Sojourner, there's a little weevil in it."
> Now I hear talk about the Constitution and the rights of man. I come up and I take hold of this Constitution. It looks mighty big. And I

> feel for my rights. But they aren't there. Then I say, "God, what ails this Constitution?" And you know what He says to me? "Sojourner, there's a little weevil in it."

She went on smoking for some years. Reproached by a foe of tobacco who said that the breath of one who smokes is bad, she agreed: "Yes, child, but when I go to Heaven I expect to leave my breath behind." Not long after, she gave up the habit.

She was born on the farm of a Col. Johannes Hardenbergh, a prosperous Dutch patroon in Ulster County, New York, west of the Hudson River and about eighty miles north of New York City. Her father had been kidnapped in Africa, brought to America, and sold. Her mother was born in this country, but *her* mother had also been captured in Africa; as a child, Sojourner was taught African songs whose words neither she nor her mother understood. Her father's name was James, her mother's Elizabeth. Slaves had no surnames; they usually took that of their current owner.

She was called Isabelle (or Isabella) shortened to Belle. She was next to the last of about ten or eleven children; the older ones were sold off by Colonel Hardenbergh when they reached a suitable age, a standard practice at the time. In the South, where Negroes were in greater demand, it was widely believed, whether true or not, that some plantation owners made a large share of their income from the sale of the offspring of their human property. The parents had to sit by helpless while their small children were seized and carried away; the general theory among the white people was that the victims did not share the love of their children that Caucasians had. This was part of a general myth of inferiority; the Negro was said to have a smaller cranial capacity than other races, and therefore be doomed to a low level of intelligence, in spite of the obvious fact that some of them were brilliant.

As to love of children, Isabelle knew better. She heard her parents tell over and over, in anguish, of the kidnapping of the two children next older than herself, a boy of five and a girl of three. It was midwinter; the slave buyers came in a sleigh, and when the boy saw them take his little sister and put her into a box on the sleigh, he knew something was wrong. He ran through the snow as fast as his little legs would go, trying to find somewhere to hide. Not to his parents; he already knew they were powerless to help him. He was caught and carried off screaming.

Colonel Hardenbergh died, and his small number of slaves were inherited by his son. The Colonel had treated them reasonably well, but his son had a different temper. He bought a new house a few miles away, and put the slaves, men, women, children, whether related or not, into one large room—as was the custom. It was a cellar, with no floor, only planks laid side by side on the dirt, which in wet weather turned to mud. It is not surprising that Isabelle's father, like others, soon contracted severe rheumatism.

In a few years the son of Colonel Hardenbergh also died, and his estate was auctioned off, including

Isabelle. But her parents were not included in the sale.

Before 1785, New York State required any owner setting a slave free to deposit a substantial sum with the town treasury, in case the freedman should become a public charge. In that year this provision was canceled; the intention was kindly, but the result was sometimes disastrous. Owners would turn off their aged or ailing slaves to shift for themselves; this was in fact a violation of the law, but one often overlooked.

James was by now severely crippled, and the owners of the estate set him and his wife free, on the theory that she could look after him. But unluckily, she died before he did, and he ended up living alone in desperate circumstances in a cabin in the woods. There his body was found one day.

Isabelle, aged nine at the time of the auction, was bought by a farmer, for $100; as she remembered it, no one would bid on her, and a few sheep were thrown in to make the bargain attractive. The new owner was John Neely, and his wife promptly made her do as much work as she was able; this was one of several wives of owners who went out of their way to be cruel to the slave girl. Since Isabelle spoke only her bastard Dutch dialect, and the Neelys spoke English, naturally she often failed to understand their orders. Because of this, John took her to the barn, tied her hands behind her back, and whipped her mercilessly; she bore the scars the rest of her life.

When she was thirteen, she was bought by Martin Schryver, an easygoing saloonkeeper on the river. He in turn sold her not long after to John J. Dumont of the town of New Paltz, and with him she remained for many years. He was not a bad master—he only beat her occasionally—but his wife was one of the cruel ones.

When she was in her late teens, she met and fell in love with a slave from a neighboring farm, named Bob. But he stole over to see her, and his master objected; he was caught, and beaten so badly that his life was probably shortened; he died not long after.

Some time later, Isabelle was married to another slave, named Tom. He had had two other wives, but no one seemed to know what had become of them. In the course of a few years, they had five children, some of whom were sold.

In 1817, as reported, New York State passed a law freeing all slaves over forty. If you were under forty you had to serve another ten years. (The situation was complicated; an earlier law set women slaves free when they reached twenty-five, men at twenty-eight.) Because she was a hard and eager worker, Mr. Dumont agreed to give Isabelle her freedom at the end of nine years, instead of ten; but when the time came, he went back on his promise. She had had an injured hand for some months, which interfered with her work, and he used this as an excuse. Furious at this double-dealing, she took a hazardous step; she ran away. She had heard of a family some miles distant who were against slavery, and sought refuge with them, with her youngest baby in her arms. They welcomed her warmly, and she slept in a bed for the first time in her life; she was about twenty-nine.

Mr. Dumont, outraged, came charging after her.

The family with whom she had sought refuge placated him by buying the last year of her time for $20, and the potential services of her baby, for $5.

Freedom for the slaves in New York State was only about two years away, when Mr. Dumont sold Isabelle's four-year-old son, Peter. Technically he could not sell him for life, under the law, but his labor could be sold until he was twenty-eight; and if he should be illegally smuggled out of the state, into the South, as was not uncommon, he would of course spend the rest of his days in bondage. Isabelle protested desperately to Mr. Dumont and his wife, but both were adamant. Mrs. Dumont, as she remembered long afterward, sneered at her for making "such a fuss about a little nigger," pointing out that she had other children, not yet sold, who were all she could care for.

Her fears were realized; Peter was passed from one owner to another, to a man who promptly took him to Alabama. His mother was heartbroken, though her black friends all agreed there was nothing she could do.

But Isabelle did something. With courage unimaginable for a black slave in that day, she complained to the law. To sell a slave in New York for illegal transportation outside the state was subject to severe penalties. The man who had done this, Solomon Gedney, got frightened, went to Alabama, and brought the child back. When he was returned, the terrified boy had been coached by his owner to say he did not recognize Isabelle as his mother, and wanted to stay with his master. With great difficulty, she finally got him to her home. When she examined him, his back was a mass of scars from top to bottom from the beatings he had received, as terrible as those on his mother's own back, inflicted many years earlier. The man in Alabama proved to be a half-insane sadist; a little later, he killed his wife with his bare hands. Ironically, she was the sister of Solomon Gedney.

Freedom came at last to the slaves in New York State, and a new life opened up to Isabelle. She earned her living as a domestic, but now she could work anywhere she chose. Tom, her husband, many years older than herself, had been put into the poorhouse, miles away. She decided to go to New York City, where in spite of the difficulties, Peter might find an education. She did so, remaining there for more than a decade.

Her feeling of piety had been growing deeper with the passage of time, and in New York she soon found for herself a circle of people, nearly all of them white, who shared her views. Before long, she had joined a religious commune, of the sort common in those days. Unluckily it shared the faults of such groupings, then and now. There was a leader who claimed to be God's vicar, or sometimes God himself; devoted followers who gave him all their money; luxurious living on his part—especially after the commune moved to Ossining, a few miles north on the bank of the Hudson; sexual irregularities, with the leader as chief of a harem. In the case of this group, there was also a mysterious death of a man believed to have been poisoned. The leader of the cult was tried for murder but acquitted for lack of conclusive evidence. When two other members, a man and wife, said that Isabelle was implicated, she again showed enormous courage for a black woman in a white man's world. She sued for slander, and got a verdict in her favor, with damages in the huge amount, for those times and circumstances, of $125. Chastened by her experience, she went back to New York and to housework.

There Peter learned to read and write, as she had hoped; but over the years, he became wayward. Planning to make a career for him at sea, she put him into a school that taught navigation, but he was a truant so many times he was expelled. Finally, in his teens, she found him a place in the crew of a whaler out of Nantucket. He wrote her infrequently, from far distant places in the South Seas; friends read his letters to her. Then they ceased, and she never heard of him again.

In 1843, when she was forty-six, there occurred in her one of the most remarkable changes in personality on record, as amazing as that which turned Joan of Arc, whom she in some ways resembled, from a simple peasant girl to a military and political leader. Always deeply religious, Isabelle had begun to commune with God more and more. On June first of that year, she received what she believed to be a Divine command to leave New York and travel on the Lord's errands. At the same time, she felt she was told to change her name from Isabelle to Sojourner. From that day forward the shy and lonely, frightened slave girl and anxious mother became a strong, self-confident public figure. She told her friend, Mrs. Whiting, for whom she was doing housework as usual, that she must go, and must travel east.

"What are you going east for?"

"The Spirit calls me there, and I must go."

She packed a few items of clothing into a pillow-case, put some food into a basket, and started out, with twenty-five cents. She began prosaically by taking the ferry to Brooklyn, and walked on from there. When night fell, she had gone a few miles, and found shelter with a hospitable family. This was to be her pattern for many months; sometimes she worked a few days for money, sometimes she paid for her overnight lodging with help in the house, at which she had had nearly forty years' training. She encountered race prejudice; she met bad characters who sought to do her harm; but on the whole, people—nearly all, of course, white—were friendly and hospitable.

Everywhere she went, she found religious meetings being held; it was an era of such things. She would slip quietly into the room, join in the singing, and when it was time for individuals to testify, she would rise and speak. When she did so, a wonderful thing happened; instantly there was dead silence, every head turned toward her. She had the magic power of personality that no one has ever been able to explain, but everyone recognizes. Soon word of her powers ran ahead of her in her travels, and she was eagerly welcomed when she appeared.

Early in her travels, a woman asked her name, and when she answered "Sojourner," was asked, "Don't you have another?" Instantly, as though God were guiding her, she answered, "It is Truth." An appropriate name for one who, as she said, felt she was called "to testify of the hope that is in me," to ask people to repent, abjure sin, and embrace Jesus.

From Long Island she went, after some time, to New England by way of a boat to Bridgeport, Connecticut. By now, people were sending her to friends farther on, with letters which she could not read, but which vouched for her. In time she came to Northampton, roughly in the center of Massachusetts, and there she joined another commune and settled down. It was not a sleazy, corrupt affair like the one at Ossining; it resembled Brook Farm or Bronson Alcott's Fruitlands. The members, surprisingly, raised silkworms, and wove and sold their silk. They were strong Abolitionists, and now for the first time Sojourner became aware that there were many white people concerned about the wretched state of the slaves, and trying to do something about it. She felt the Lord had called her there, and joined their efforts with a full heart.

In Northampton occurred a dangerous episode which also showed her power to command respect in unlikely quarters. A religious camp meeting was being held nearby, with nightly revival services, and Sojourner attended. One night a rowdy mob of Northampton youths descended upon the meeting with the intention to destroy the camp and chase away those who were there. It was a rough and dangerous era, and all their lives were in some danger, but Sojourner's, as the only black present, most of all. In a momentary panic, she started to run away, but then her faith rose up in her, and she halted. The crowd was in turmoil, the attackers and the attacked mixed up together. Sojourner found a little hill, and began to sing in her deep, powerful voice, her favorite hymn, dealing with the Resurrection.

It was early in the morning—it was early in the morning,
Just at the break of day—
When He rose—when He rose—when He rose,
And went to heaven on a cloud.

The effect was magical. The young roisterers came where she was, and clustered close around her, so close that she cried out, "Why do you come about me with clubs and sticks? I am not doing harm to anyone."

"We aren't going to hurt you, old woman; we came to hear you sing," someone said. And others added, "Sing to us, old woman." "Talk to us." Since the crowd could not all see her, they suggested she stand in a wagon nearby. She protested that hotheads would overthrow it, and the leaders assured her they would see this did not happen. So she talked.

> There are two congregations on this ground. It is written that there shall be a separation, and the sheep shall be separated from the goats. The other preachers have the sheep, I have the goats. And I have a few sheep among my goats, but they are very ragged.

In cold type, it does not sound like much, but it worked. They roared with laughter, began asking her questions, listened to her answers, asked her to sing again. Finally she made them promise that with one more song they would go and leave her—and the camp meeting—in peace. So she sang one final hymn.

I bless the Lord I've got my seal—today and today—
    To slay Goliath in the field—today and today;
The good old way is a righteous way,
    I mean to take the kingdom in the good old way.

The young horde of mischief makers then departed quietly, leaving the members of the camp meeting to marvel at Sojourner's power.

The Abolitionists soon realized what a jewel they had in her. Here was a woman who had been a cruelly abused slave for the first thirty years of her life, who was at the same time a commanding platform presence. William Lloyd Garrison and other leaders soon became her friends, and began sending her on speaking tours with one or the other of their members.

This was dangerous work. We tend to forget nowadays that there were many sympathizers with the South, and with the institution of slavery, in the North. During the Civil War they had to go more or less underground, and were called Copperheads. Sojourner once remarked, during that period, "Years ago, my occupation was scouring brass doorknobs; but now I go about scouring Copperheads." She was in triple jeopardy, as an Abolitionist, as a woman, and as a black.

Time and time again, she and the other Abolitionists who shared the platform with her had to be rescued by the police. Some states—Indiana was one—had laws forbidding even a free black to cross their borders; she ignored these laws, but they made her position even more difficult. In one town, the Copperheads threatened, "If that nigger, Sojourner Truth, tries to speak in the Town Hall, we'll burn the building." Said Sojourner, "Then I'll speak upon its ashes." The building remained intact. When she was arrested by a Copperhead sheriff, and was about to be hauled off to jail, she was rescued by a Union Army officer, who claimed she was his prisoner instead. On one occasion she was arrested and tried, but the prosecuting attorney was so drunk that the whole affair fell apart in court.

In 1850 came the terrible Fugitive Slave Law. Before that, a runaway from the South could attain a sort of uneasy safety if he could get into a Northern state, though there were many kidnappings there. But the new law, passed as a sop to the South in the dispute over whether the new lands in the West should be free or slave, destroyed that safety. Extending and strengthening a law of 1793, it commanded all citizens to aid the federal marshals in the pursuit and capture of a runaway. Once caught he was brought before a federal commissioner, where he was not allowed to testify in his own behalf, while any written or oral statement by his alleged owner was accepted as gospel. The commissioners got twice the fee if the slave was returned to the South. Under this rule some free Negroes were arrested and taken South, in real or pretended cases of "mistaken identity." Frederick Douglass, the most famous man of his race, did not dare walk alone in the poor part of any city, lest this happen to him.

The new law exacerbated the storm that was rising between North and South, which was to end in war eleven years later. In some places, mobs of angry citizens broke into jails to set Negroes free; sometimes countermobs of Copperheads fought them. Some Northern states passed local laws defying the new federal statute.

There is today a revisionist school of historians who say that the popular myth about the horrors of slavery is exaggerated, as to quantity if not quality. No doubt they are right; all popular myths tend to exaggeration. But something must have been terribly wrong, apart from the profound moral flaw in any society where some are free and others are not, or so many would not have tried the desperate expedient of running away, often pursued with dogs and guns, and subject to dreadful punishment if caught.

The proportion of sadistically minded people, who inflicted brutal punishment without compunction, may very well have been about the same in the North as in the South. Some slaves were well treated, in both areas, before the institution was abolished. The moral climate of the day condoned severe physical punishment; schoolboys were whipped. Sojourner, her small son, and her sweetheart, Bob, were among the unlucky ones.

Conditions were in general worse in the South, for several reasons. In the North most people had no slaves, and very rarely did anyone own more than a small number. In the South, also, most people had no slaves, and of those who did, the majority owned only a few. But on the Southern plantations, large numbers were held. Here the house servants, who came into direct contact with the white owners, were usually well treated, except as to concubinage. It was the field hands who suffered the most. Allan Nevins, in his monumental eight-volume work, *Ordeal of the Union,* summarizes what went on. The big plantations employed overseers, who were almost always more cruel than the owners; the harder they worked the slaves, the higher their pay. In South Carolina, the law provided for a fifteen-hour workday, but this was impossible to enforce, and usually "from can see to can't see," from dawn to dark, was the rule. To hurry the workers into the field, an overseer would administer a beating to the last to arrive.

Particularly severe was the lot of slaves who were leased to a second party. Usually, the rule was that a slave should be fed and treated well enough to enable him to work hard, but sometimes the lessee found it more profitable to underfeed and overwork such slaves, regardless of whether they died. So common was this practice that Jefferson, forced for financial reasons to rent out some slaves, put a clause in the contract stipulating that even though some died, the amount to be paid was to be the same. As he wrote, "Otherwise, it would be their interest to kill all the old and infirm by hard usage."

Some Negro families certainly were broken up, the members being sold individually to distant places, perhaps never to see each other again. Jefferson sold a few slaves to rectify such conditions, and Ralph Waldo Emerson, on a sojourn in St. Augustine, heard such an auction going on through a thin wall while sitting in a religious service.

As the Civil War grew nearer, tension in the South mounted to the point of hysteria, and the lot of freed Negroes became ever harder. Louisiana and Arkansas forbade ships to traverse their waters if they had freedmen among the crew. Finally these two states ordered all free Negroes to be expelled by a specified date; they had to sell their property for whatever it would bring. But there was a loophole: The freedman could sell himself into lifelong slavery, and in that case, he got half the money, the state taking the other half.

Civil rights were almost nonexistent in the South, and precarious in the North. In the slave states, even a free Negro was barred, as noted, from most of the professions and some occupations. He could not vote, or testify in court. He had to carry on his person at all times proof of his free status, lest he be seized and sold to some distant point. In some states, of which Maryland was one, a Negro convicted of a crime would be leased by the state to a slave owner for a period of years; if the owner was in the Deep South, the individual often disappeared forever. A second conviction in Maryland sometimes resulted in being sold for life. In some Southern states, slaves were forbidden to save money and buy their own freedom;

this was in any case difficult, since the going rate, which was $500 or $600 at the beginning of the nineteenth century, rose to $1,500 to $2,000 in the 1850s. Sometimes an owner was forbidden to free his slaves in his will.

In the North, where slavery had finally been abolished only thirty years earlier, there were many restrictions in the 1850s. Most schools were closed to Negro children, and most occupations except the most menial were barred, by cultural pattern if not by law. In addition to Indiana, Negroes were forbidden to settle in Illinois, Iowa, or Oregon, and there was social pressure against them in other states. Oregon, in its Constitution of 1857, actually disfranchised Negro citizens already there. Almost universally, they were not admitted to membership in white Protestant churches, just as they were excluded from places of public entertainment, or confined to the rear of the room or a balcony. They were forbidden to vote, or severely restricted, in all Northern states but three—Massachusetts, Maine, and New Hampshire. A common handicap was the requirement that the would-be voter must own $250 in land, a large sum in those days, and especially for an unskilled worker.

The increased tension in the South produced the Underground Railroad, with its hundreds of heroic men and women who at heavy risk helped slaves to escape to the North and to Canada. One of Sojourner's friends was the greatly admired escaped slave, Harriet Tubman. Ignoring the danger, Harriet went back into the South *nineteen times*, leading three hundred slaves along the Underground Railroad, while the price the angry Southerners put on her head rose and rose, to a total of $40,000.

In the year of the Fugitive Slave Law, Sojourner's biography was published. It was an unpretentious little volume of 128 pages, written anonymously by a white friend, Olive Gilbert, who lived in Northampton. It lies before me on my table. The prose seems somewhat florid and quaint today (as ours will seem a century and a quarter from now), but it told the story as Sojourner, with her marvelous memory, recalled it. Since she of course did not know how to spell any of the names, most of them are wrong; modern research has corrected them. Oddly enough, while the book itself seems touched by time, the quotations from Sojourner do not.

The volume, entitled *Narrative of Sojourner Truth: A Northern Slave,* was not distributed to bookstores. William Lloyd Garrison wrote an introduction, and guaranteed the cost of publication, and the first edition, of a few hundred copies, was delivered to Sojourner herself. From then on, she sold the book at all her public meetings, using the small difference between the cost and the retail price to reimburse the printer, to make payments on a small house that had been built for her in Northampton, and to live on. When the first edition was exhausted, another was prepared. When this one was all gone, Sojourner, presumably feeling that she had saturated her market, switched to copies of her own photograph; since they cost less, they sold faster. She called the picture "my shadow," and always said, "I sell the shadow to support the substance."

I am looking at that picture as I write. Sojourner is seated by a little table with a small bouquet of flowers on it; she is wearing a white shawl and a white turban, and facing into the camera. I may be reading too much into a photograph, but her expression suggests to me a wry recognition that life is difficult, plus a determination to do her best with it nevertheless.

Very early in her public career, people began to ask for copies of her songs. There weren't any; she had written them in her head, words and music, and there they had remained. But friends wrote them down for her, they were printed on single sheets, and she sold these, too, for a few pennies. One of the favorites with the public, which had many verses, began:

> I am pleading for my people,
> A poor downtrodden race,
> Who dwell in freedom's boasted land,
> With no abiding place.

In 1878, when she was probably eighty-one, she was in especially straitened circumstances. Another friend, Frances Titus, of Battle Creek, Michigan, got out a new edition of the *Narrative* for Sojourner, this one telling the rest of her story up to that time. From 128 pages it was now expanded to 320. In the early 1860s, she had begun to carry with her an autograph book which she called her "Book of Life," and before she died, it had a number of the names of famous people—William Lloyd Garrison, Wendell Phillips, Lucretia Mott, and many more. Some were reproduced in the new edition of the *Narrative*.

Among the signatures was that of President Lincoln. When he signed the Emancipation Proclamation, she felt she had to go and see him. It was a serious journey for a woman of sixty-six, who by now was in rather frail health, but she set forth. Her route was roundabout, and her progress so leisurely that it was many months before she arrived. When she and the President met, she told him with her invariable honesty, "I never heard of you before you were talked of for President."

"Well, I heard of you, years and years before I thought of being President," was his answer. "Your name was well known in the Middle West." And he signed her Book of Life:

> "For Aunty Sojourner Truth,
> Oct. 29, 1864 A. Lincoln

While she was in Washington, she once decided to visit the Senate, where twenty or more of the members crowded around her to shake her hand, and fourteen of them signed her book. Among them was Charles Sumner of Massachusetts, a hero of the Abolitionist movement. Another signed simply, "H. R. Revels, Senator, Mississippi, Colored."

When the Emancipation Proclamation was signed, even though the War would continue for another sixteen months, thousands of Negro families fled from nearby slave states to Washington, where they crowded together in miserable hovels not far from where the Bonus Army lived nearly seventy years later in the Presidency of Herbert Hoover. They were ignorant and helpless, they and their surroundings were very dirty, and Sojourner, to whom cleanliness had been one of the first laws of life since she was a girl, volunteered to help them. She was put on the government payroll, stayed more than two years—and then spent five more years trying to collect the salary she had been promised—$15 a month.

Slave traders from Virginia and Maryland were entering the camps and stealing small children; Sojourner fought them to a standstill. When a proslavery marshal threatened her with arrest, she answered, "If you do, I'll make the United States rock like a cradle."

On another occasion, when an officer challenged her with "Who are you, old woman?" she answered, "I am that I am," and walked away, leaving the bemused policeman scratching his head.

Sojourner was the first Freedom Rider. In Washington in those days most of the (horsedrawn) omnibuses were reserved for white people; the blacks usually had to walk. Time after time, Sojourner, with great difficulty, managed to get on board a vehicle, and outfaced the conductor who wanted to put her off. When she completed such a journey, she walked down the street shouting, "Praise God! I've had a ride!" One conductor shoved her so hard her shoulder was dislocated. With enormous courage, she had him arrested, convicted, and dismissed, to the undoubted outrage of most of his fellows; after all, he had only attacked an old Negro woman.

Sojourner, who sensibly saw that economic independence must go with political freedom, worked hard, with the wide contacts she now had throughout the North, to get jobs for emancipated slaves. This activity soon codified itself into a dream of a huge resettlement program in Kansas, where she hoped as many as three million former slaves might, with government help, establish new lives for themselves. She campaigned ceaselessly for this project for years, but it was not to be. "Reconstruction" had begun, and the nation was absorbed in other things.

Her interest in improving the lot of women began almost as soon as she settled in Northampton, when she first came into contact with such outstanding leaders of the movement as Susan B. Anthony, Emma Willard, Lucretia Mott, and Elizabeth Cady Stanton. Believing as she did in justice for all, it would have been impossible for her to stand aloof.

The legal and cultural position of women in the 1850s was even worse than many women felt it was in the 1970s. A woman was to all effects the ward of her father until she became the ward of her husband. In most places, she had no property rights at all; if she earned anything it went to her male guardian, father or husband. Similarly, she had no rights in respect to her children. While there were plenty of female seminaries, only one institution of higher learning—Oberlin College—was available without question to women who could meet its academic standards. Most of the professions, and nearly all other occupations except household work, were barred, by law or by custom.

Public opinion (mostly male) was more bitter than it was (in the North) against Abolitionists, and Sojourner was thus doubly vulnerable. Sometimes she tried pleading: "If my cup won't hold but a pint, and yours holds a quart, wouldn't you be mean not to let me have my little half-measure full?" Sometimes she was firmer. When a heckler shouted triumphantly, "Christ wasn't a woman!" Sojourner answered: "Where did Christ come from? From God and a woman. Man had nothing to do with him."

On occasion she was enigmatic. To the charge that Eve had ruined everything by tempting Adam with an apple and getting them expelled from the Garden of Eden, she said, "If the first woman was strong enough to turn the world upside down, women together must be able to turn it back."

Another heckler said contemptuously, "I don't care any more for your talk than I do for the bite of a flea."

Sojourner: "Perhaps not, but the Lord willing, I'll keep you scratching."

She would not let herself be entangled in theological sophistries. When a Seventh-Day Adventist challenged her, "Don't you believe that the Lord is coming?" Sojourner said, "I believe the Lord is as near as He can be, and not be *it*."

Her faith in miracles was of course absolute, but she expressed it in her own way. When a boy fell off a milldam, but lit in a narrow water area and was unharmed, she commented, "If the devil made him fall, the Lord had fixed a place for him to light in."

Her hard life as a girl helped her in arguing with those who said women were too delicate for the rough-and-tumble of politics. When one such observed that "women must be helped into carriages and over puddles," Sojourner's caustic answer was,

"Nobody ever helps me into carriages, or over mud puddles, or gives me any best place—and aren't I a woman?"

The rumor that she was in fact a man, which began because of her deep voice, continued for years. The basis was supposed (by males) to be a left-handed compliment, the idea being that only a man could display such power of intellect. Finally, at a large public meeting, a committee (all men, you may be sure) came up on the platform, and demanded that she retire with them and prove her femininity by showing her breast. Said Sojourner: "I will show my breast, but to the entire congregation." She did so, adding, "It is not my shame, but yours, that I do this." The rumors stopped.

By the 1850s, Sojourner's four daughters, Diana, Hannah, Elizabeth, and Sophia, were all grown, married, scattered, and some with children of their own. Hannah's son James was a bright boy, a favorite of his grandmother, and she took him on some of her travels. When Harriet Beecher Stowe published *Uncle Tom's Cabin*, Sojourner felt she had to meet the author, and with characteristic directness and simplicity, she went to visit her, taking James. Harriet was charmed, and so was the famous minister, Lyman Beecher, her father, who was staying with his daughter at the time. Sojourner told the story of her life to Harriet, who made notes on it, and nearly a decade later, published an article about her, "The Libyan Sibyl," in *The Atlantic Monthly*. This of course spread her fame much farther than the few hundred copies of her biography that she had sold. Said Harriet: "I do not recollect ever to have been conversant with anyone who had more of that silent and subtle power which we call personal presence."

Her curious title came from the fact that, in the interval, she had told Sojourner's story to a famous sculptor of the day, John Ward. Without ever seeing Sojourner, he made a statue of her as "the Libyan Sibyl," which was exhibited at a World's Fair, and got much attention.

While Sojourner composed the music as well as the words of some of her songs, she also on occasion used the compositions of others. She sang for Harriet and her father a song to the tune of Stephen Foster's "Oh, Susannah."

> I'm on my way to Canada,
> That cold, but happy, land;
> The dire effects of slavery
> I can no longer stand.
>
> Oh, righteous Father,
> Do look down on me,
> And help me on to Canada,
> Where colored folks are free.

In 1856, Sojourner moved to Battle Creek, soon followed by her daughter Hannah, and James. Quaker friends of hers had moved there some time earlier. The Dred Scott case was before the Supreme Court, and a few months later came the terrible decision that a liberated man, if he ventured back into slave territory, lost his freedom. Free Negroes were being kidnapped in the North and rushed South. While Battle Creek is not very far north of the Indiana state line, there was an open passage to Canada there; it was in fact an important station on the Underground Railroad.

Sojourner of course used her new home only as a momentary resting place between her speaking tours. She went up and down the country ceaselessly, speaking for freedom for blacks, for women, for everybody. Alcohol was a dreadful evil in that day, and she added temperance to her crusade. Conditions in prisons were frightful, and she urged reform of the penal system.

When the Civil War began, a big training camp for the Union Army was set up at Detroit, and Sojourner flung herself into helping the bewildered, frightened young men who were learning there to be soldiers. Soon the war came to have a more personal meaning to her; Hannah's James, now old enough to fight, enlisted in the all-Negro Fifty-fourth Massachusetts Regiment. Soon it was in a fierce battle at Fort Wagner, South Carolina, and James was reported missing in action. But Hannah and Sojourner never gave up, and sure enough, James was spotted marching with his regiment in a victory parade after the war.

With the end of hostilities came the end of slavery; but there was still an enormous amount for Sojourner to do for her people, helping settle those uprooted by the conflict, helping to move many of them from the sixteenth into the nineteenth century. She worked long and hard on her project for a great colony in Kansas, and was sad when it came to nothing. And always, there were her crusading speeches for women's rights, for temperance, and for prison reform.

As the 1860s came to a close, and she entered her own seventies, she was, in addition to her national fame, a well-known character in Battle Creek. Her Quaker friend, Charles Merritt, owned a blackberry patch, and Sojourner helped pick the berries, and then peddled them from house to house, a big tray, with the small boxes on it, balanced on her head. But by now she had learned the value of publicity; she sent another grandson, Sammy, the day before to go down the chosen streets with a few handbills to announce her coming. With the berries, the bemused residents got some of her wit and wisdom, and a few words on behalf of her favorite causes.

She was still erect, and her skin was smooth. When she met her friend Lucretia Mott, now herself elderly, at a women's rights convention, Lucretia said to her, "How can it be that I am so wrinkled, and your face is as smooth as can be?" Said Sojourner: "I have two skins, a white one under, and a black one to cover it."

But she was not as well as she seemed. She now had periods of severe illness, especially an ulcerated leg. The Merritts took her into their home, and when she ran out of money, a public appeal was made, and funds came in from all parts of the North. Her doctor was J. H. Kellogg, who survives today only as a bold signature on boxes of cereal; but he was a skillful physician, and he kept her alive until her eighty-sixth year. Her ulcerated leg needed a skin graft; when the frightened members of her family refused to help, Dr. Kellogg is reported to have used some of his own skin; amazingly, it was not rejected by her body, and the ulcer healed.

When she died, in 1883, leading white citizens of Battle Creek were proud to be her pallbearers. Her grave, a simple marble shaft in a little clearing with cypresses around it, is still visited by large numbers of pilgrims. Her death was accompanied by an outpouring of tributes to her from the survivors of her own generation who remembered what she had done. Said Frederick Douglass: "Venerable for age, distinguished for insight into human nature, remarkable for independence and courageous self-assertion, devoted to the welfare of her race, she has been for the last forty years an object of respect and admiration for social reformers everywhere." But I like better the words of Mrs. L. H. Pearson, one of her friends, otherwise unknown to fame, who said, "Sojourner Truth is the most marvelous person we have ever had the pleasure of meeting."

She spoke of her songs as "home made"; and I think of Sojourner herself as a home-made miracle. She would have said that God played an important part in what she achieved; and many today will probably agree with her. But beyond such speculation, we must not forget the genes she inherited from her African ancestors. It is impossible not to believe that from somewhere in those lost generations in the dark forest came a contribution to the power and dignity that were hers.

five

Ralph Waldo Emerson: The First American Scholar

RALPH WALDO EMERSON was a towering American genius, a poet, philosopher, author, lecturer, a man whose message to the world is as valuable today as it was a hundred years ago. From his quiet study in Concord, Massachusetts, he formulated challenging thoughts that reverberated across America and Europe. Robert Frost, himself a wise American as well as a beloved poet, calls him one of the four greatest men this country has ever produced, a peer of Washington, Lincoln, and Jefferson. Supreme Court Justice Oliver Wendell Holmes wrote in his old age that "the only firebrand of my youth that burns to me as brightly as ever is Emerson." Matthew Arnold thought that his *Essays* were "the most important work done in prose during the [nineteenth] century." Henry James, the novelist, who did not give praise lightly, said, "He had a particular faculty, which has not been surpassed, for speaking to the soul in a voice of direction and authority." Henry's brother William said that "posterity will reckon him a prophet."

Before Emerson, American students of culture were almost abject in their devotion to the Europeans. He summoned them to stand on their own feet and be their own men and did more than anyone else to loosen these bonds, and it is therefore not unfair to call him "the first American Scholar."

More clearly than anyone else, he stated the heart of the issue between democracy and the fascists or communists, who deny the worth of the individual and summon their antlike, faceless legions to the service of the state. On a lesser scale, he is the great enemy of the Organization Man; always he fought conformity and the timid yielding to your supposed superiors.

Many of his phrases have become common coin, used daily by people probably ignorant of their origin: "Hitch your wagon to a star." (A cliché today, but what a shining image when first minted!) "An institution is the lengthened shadow of one man." "Nothing great was ever achieved without enthusiasm." "A foolish consistency is the hobgoblin of little minds." "To be great is to be misunderstood." "Things are in the saddle, and ride mankind." "The less government we have, the better." "Wherever Macdonald sits, there is the head of the table." (Usually misquoted as "MacGregor.") "When half-gods go, the gods arrive." "What torments of grief you endured/ From evils that never arrived!" Sometimes he sounds like Thoreau: "A man builds a fine house, and now he has a master, and a task for life; he is to furnish, watch, show it, and keep it in repair the rest of his days."

Among his poems are the enduring "Concord Hymn," which used to be known to every schoolboy: "Here once the embattled farmers stood/ And fired the shot heard round the world," and his summons to self-confidence: "When Duty whispers low, *Thou must*/ The youth replies, *I can*."

For many years, on any fine spring or autumn day, he could be found haunting the Boston docks, joining some knot of momentarily idle sailors or longshoremen, drawing out their views on many matters. In the winter of 1832–33, crossing the stormy Atlantic in a tiny vessel of only 236 tons, he was on deck when most of the passengers were seasick in their cabins, talking to the seamen while trying not very successfully to keep out of their way. Later in his tiny, cramped quarters, he recorded in his journal their untutored philosophy. Late into his life, he would roll up his sleeves and try clumsily to help the farmhands in the fields, for the chance to talk to them. When he traveled, he sat by preference in the cheapest seat, to chat with the humbler of his fellow passengers. Asked to make a speech on a college campus, he would find some pretext to linger on several days and mingle with the students, who were as enchanted with him as he with them.

A belief and a purpose lay behind all these activities. The belief was that every man has something to contribute to all; the purpose, to demonstrate this by actually finding out what people thought and felt, and preferably, the plain people. He mistrusted the wisdom of most "educated" men, believing that they had all too often stuffed their heads so full of the records of the dusty past that they left no room for their own thoughts. It was this attitude which helped him to be venerated as a sage before he was forty, with thousands of persons making pilgrimages to his home in Concord and millions, all over the world, for more than a century, taking comfort and inspiration from his words.

He rejoiced when a commoner outsmarted a college graduate—even though the graduate was himself. Once he stood outside his own cow stable trying to persuade a largish heifer calf to go in. The calf didn't want to, and the more her owner pushed and tugged, the more rocklike she stood, feet apart, not budging.

In this impasse, an Irish-born servant girl happened by. Without a word, she put her finger into the calf's mouth; "seduced by this maternal imitation," as someone afterward told the story, the animal readily followed her into the stable. Emerson was delighted. He put the incident into his journal that day, adding, "I like people who can do things." It was a sentiment that was to recur hundreds of times in the ten big volumes of the journal that have survived and are today in print.

His admiration for practical people arose partly from his own incompetence in routine affairs of life. He could not pack a trunk, or drive a nail straight. From time to time he would go into his garden with a shovel and attack the soil furiously, to work off steam, or perhaps to show he was a man among men (as he had never been a boy among boys). On one such occasion, his small son Waldo watched him for a few minutes and then observed, "Look out, father! You'll dig your leg!"

Born in 1803 in Boston, the fourth of five sons, with only one sister, descended from six generations of New England ministers, Emerson lived all his life in poverty, especially severe after his father died when the boy was eight; for a time he and one of his brothers had only one overcoat between them. He worked his way through Harvard waiting on table in a dormitory, where he had to report the name of the student who broke a dish—or pay for it himself. Though he was considered an indifferent student by the standards of that day, graduating thirtieth in a class of fifty-nine, before he left college he had read and assimilated the works of twenty great classic writers of antiquity and learned five languages.

Two things about Emerson have been common to many great men. One of these is bad health in youth (he had weak lungs and eye trouble). Perhaps the willpower required to conquer such a handicap carried over and helped him. The second is that as a small child, Emerson was treated by those about him as though he were an adult; this was especially true of his Aunt Mary Emerson, the chief intellectual influence in his life after the death of his father.

After leaving Harvard the youth studied desultorily for the ministry. At twenty-six he married; his wife died of tuberculosis only two years later. At thirty-two he entered into a second marriage that was to last his lifetime and resulted in four children.

He spent a few years as a schoolteacher and a few more as a minister, but was unhappy in both vocations. In a day when school discipline for boys meant merciless beating, Emerson was notable for his light punishments. Fixing the culprit with gentle eyes he would murmur, "Oh, sad!" and assign him to read and report on some pages of Plutarch.

In the year of his second marriage he made a decision that required tremendous courage: To spend the rest of his life in the expression of pure thought, and to rely on this activity somehow to earn a living for himself and his family. Shortly before, he had managed to buy a house in Concord, a few miles northwest of Boston, and there he lived until his death at seventy-nine. From his quiet study for half a century he launched explosive thoughts; Russian students were sent by the Tsar's government to Siberia for being caught with Emerson's books in their possession. By the 1850s it was generally agreed that the minds of thoughtful men everywhere were most deeply influenced by three individuals: Carlyle, Goethe, and most of all, the sage of Concord.

Though his life was, on the whole, outwardly

uneventful, it was not without its share of tragedy. The death of his first wife was a hard blow, followed quickly by the passing of two dearly loved brothers. When he was thirty-eight, he lost his first-born son, little Waldo, and never got over it. Hearing that the boy was ill, Bronson Alcott sent his eight-year-old daughter, Louisa May, to ring the bell and find out how Waldo was. Emerson himself answered the door; the child took one look at his stricken face, turned away without speaking, and returned home to report that Waldo was dead.

Nearly all of Emerson's income came from lecturing and writing, though his first wife had left an estate which brought in a small annual sum; the amount fluctuated since he invested much of it in railroad stocks whose earnings varied greatly and sometimes disappeared. Nearly every winter for forty years he made a long, exhausting lecture tour throughout the Northeast and, later, the Middle West. His lifelong principle of never haggling over money meant that he received far less than his popularity over the years would have justified. When asked what he charged, he replied with a stock joke: "I lecture only for F.A.M.E.—Fifty and My Expenses," and this was often literally true. Publishers also took advantage of him; his books, never best sellers, brought in only $600 or $700 a year.

On four occasions he had to cross the Mississippi in winter to fulfill a lecture engagement at points where there was no bridge; three times he walked across the frozen surface, and once he was rowed over in a small and overloaded craft amid the ice floes. Even more risky was an episode in Niagara Falls where he was in a wooden hotel that burned down, escaping with only his clothes and losing his precious railroad ticket to Chicago; he was in despair until he chanced to meet an old acquaintance, a railroad man who was able to write him a pass.

While his philosophy appealed to mature and thoughtful people, his personality charmed almost everybody. A scrubwoman who always came when he lectured in his hometown of Concord confessed that she didn't understand a word, "but I like to go and see him stand up there and look as though he thought everyone was as good as he is." When he spoke in East Lexington, a lady in the audience remarked, "We are a very simple people and can understand no one but Mr. Emerson." His charm was so great that a Methodist minister remarked, "If Emerson went to hell, he would change the climate there, and emigration would set that way."

William James, Sr., father of the novelist and the psychologist, described the beginning of a lecture by Emerson, who all his life was unable to speak extemporaneously, and wrote out and read aloud every word. Says James:

> His deferential entrance upon the scene, his look of inquiry at the desk and the chair, his resolute rummaging among his embarrassed papers, the air of sudden recollection with which he would plunge into his pockets for what he must have known had never been put there, his uncertainty and irresolution as he

> rose to speak, his deep, relieved inspiration as he got well from under the burning glass of his auditors' eyes and addressed himself at length to their docile ears instead: No maiden ever appealed more potently to your enamored and admiring sympathy.

In his later years his daughter became his secretary, traveled with him, and took care of him. Since he invariably shuffled the pages of his lectures into hopeless confusion, she stitched them together down one side with strong thread.

Only on a few occasions in his life was his rapport with his audience less than complete. Just before the Civil War, when he was known as a bitter-end opponent of slavery, he was actually booed and hissed off the platform by a crowd who did not share his views—in Boston, of all places. After the war he spoke at the University of Virginia, and met some hostility from Southerners who could not yet be friendly to a Yankee, though most of the trouble was that the audience was largely composed of women and noisy children, and Emerson, not feeling well that day, was almost inaudible.

But these were exceptions. When Lincoln issued the Emancipation Proclamation in 1862, Emerson appeared at a mass meeting in Boston, made an address, and read his famous "Boston Hymn," an excoriation of the South. When he came to the thrilling lines, "Who is the owner? The slave is the owner, and ever was. Pay him," the whole huge audience leaped to its feet and cheered wildly for five minutes.

If his fees were small, the admission charges were in proportion. In Iowa, one audience got an oyster supper and Emerson, both for $1. In another town where the local paper accused him of "cheating" because he cut his lecture a little short to catch a train, the admission had been twenty-five cents.

Most of Emerson's writing is not very well organized. He pours out one thought after another, frequently condensed, sometimes cryptic, and often allusive and indirect. He once remarked rather sadly, "I found when I had finished writing my lecture that it was a very good house, only the architect had unfortunately omitted the stairs."

His style derived partly from his manner of composition. Beginning as a young man in college he would get up at 5 A.M. in his unheated cubicle, bathe (breaking the ice in his water pitcher if it were winter), dress, and sit down to write his thoughts for half an hour or an hour in his "savings bank" (his journal). As the manuscript volumes grew in number, he indexed and cross-indexed his ideas, and his books were drawn from these pages. While his major works are sometimes difficult, though always rewarding, the ten volumes of the *Journals* themselves are easy and fascinating.

One test of a great man (and how often it fails!), is his neighbors' regard for him; nowhere was Emerson better loved than by those among whom he lived, who daily saw his tall and slender, black-clad form pass among them. When he settled in Concord at the age of thirty-two, newly married to his second wife, he was subjected to a mild form of hazing: He was chosen "hog-reeve," the man who had to fine anyone whose pigs were found roaming the streets. The office was a standing joke, but Emerson gravely accepted the duty, and performed it faithfully. He was a member of the village volunteer fire department, his leather buckets always standing ready by his door.

On occasion he could be solidly practical. The hanging sign in front of Deacon Parker's store had blackened with age into a shapeless blob, and no one could remember what it had originally been. After the village had debated for weeks, Emerson suggested: "Cut it down and see." It was a dried fish.

The philosopher was delighted to record the shrewd or comical remarks he heard in unexpected quarters. Traveling in the West in winter, at 28 below zero, he chuckled when the hotel clerk said "they never had cold weather—only occasional Indian Summer and coolish nights." He heard an old scamp remark of himself that he "had a fine conscience, as good as new—he'd never used it none." When a supercilious city visitor asked a farmer whether all the natives of that region went barefoot, the farmer answered, "Some on 'em does, and some on 'em minds their own business." He rejoiced when he heard a New England farmer refuse to refer to nearby mountains by their fancy Indian names, saying instead "them there rises," or when a boy in the city streets, repudiating flattery, described it as "honey pie." He remarked wistfully that the speech of common people was far more direct and effective than the circumlocutions of the educated, and wished he had the courage to use the forceful double negative ("He ain't got none").

Concord demonstrated its affection when he was

sixty-nine, and his house burned down in the early morning, the Emersons fleeing for their lives in their nightclothes. Though most of his neighbors were about as poor as he was, one and all contributed to the fund which let him go to Egypt and travel up the Nile, while his house was being rebuilt. A joke went around the village in his absence; referring to his cryptic writing, the question was asked: "What did the Sphinx say to Mr. Emerson?" Answer: "You're another!"

The day of his return was the most memorable in Concord history for decades. By now, the town had a railroad, and the whole population waited for him at the station where a triumphal welcoming arch had been erected and—unheard-of extravagance—a brass band retained at a cost of $30.

The village could not find out (without spoiling the surprise) which train he would take from Boston, so they arranged with the engineer to keep blowing his whistle as he came near. When Emerson and his daughter stepped off the train and he saw his neighbors thronged to greet him, his eyes filled with tears. "My friends!" he said, "I know that this is not a tribute to an old man and his daughter returned to their house but to the common blood of us all—one family—in Concord!"

Another test of a great man is that he attracts other great men to him, and Emerson achieved this. A single day spent with Thomas Carlyle, the gruff Scottish historian, resulted in lifelong close friendship; the American even risked, and lost, some of his own pitiful dollars trying to get Carlyle's books published in this country. The poets, John Greenleaf Whittier and William Cullen Bryant, were his friends and so was Margaret Fuller, the first famous woman intellectual in America.

Emerson started in Boston what was probably the most illustrious luncheon club in history, the Saturday Club. Nearly all its members were famous then and are famous today: Henry Wadsworth Longfellow and James Russell Lowell, the poets; Nathaniel Hawthorne, novelist and short-story writer; Louis Agassiz, the great Swiss-born zoologist and geologist; Charles A. Dana, who was to become "Dana of *The New York Sun*"; John Lothrop Motley, the historian who wrote *The Rise of the Dutch Republic*, and Oliver Wendell Holmes, Sr., preeminent in four careers: as a physician, a teacher of medicine, an essayist *(The Autocrat of the Breakfast Table)*, and the poet who wrote "Old Ironsides," "The Chambered Nautilus," and "The Wonderful One-Hoss Shay." It needed a giant to be first among such a group of giants; but not for a moment did anyone question that this was Emerson's role.

These great men were also human. When a group of them, all contributors to Lowell's newly founded *Atlantic Monthly*, were sitting at lunch, and a bundle of copies was brought in, fresh from the press, conversation stopped while each man seized a copy to read eagerly his own contribution. (Writers haven't changed much.)

Emerson himself could be laughed at on occasion. Once at a meeting he was arguing with Agassiz: "Some of us believe with Kant that time is merely a subjective form of human thought, having no objective existence." Then he looked at his watch and added hastily: "Good Heavens! The Concord train leaves in fifteen minutes!" He departed on the run, leaving the other members shaking with laughter.

The people of Concord could never understand why Emerson allowed cranks and crackpots to take up so much of his time; but this policy was in accord with his general principle that everyone has something to contribute and that we have no right to sit in judgment on others. "The charm of life is this variety of genius, these contrasts and flavors by which Heaven has modulated the identity of truth." He deplored "the perpetual hankering to violate this individuality, to warp his ways of thinking and behavior to resemble or reflect your own thinking and behavior."

Most eccentric of his circle was perhaps Bronson Alcott, with his head always in the clouds, a man who had sired a brood of daughters but would not care for them. He poured out an endless torrent of ideas to anyone who would listen, which usually meant Emerson, who once called him "a pail without any bottom." The two would start off for a long walk, but rarely got beyond the first stile, where Alcott would pause and spout his thoughts in a monologue, until it was time to turn back again. Like Emerson, he sometimes lectured, but usually forgot to arrange a fee; if he had done so, he would forget to collect it. Sent to the market to buy food for his hungry family, he would come back triumphantly with a new book instead. When a confidence man asked him for $5, Alcott handed him $10; this was too much for the swindler, who gave back the money.

With some visionary friends as impractical as himself Alcott established a cooperative farm colony, Fruitlands, where all the labor was done by the people probably most incompetent in America to do it. The group would not eat meat, fish, eggs, milk or butter or honey, or use wool or cotton. Their only sugar was from the maple; their only bread was made without yeast. One poor women was expelled for going to the house of a neighbor and eating some fish, though she pleaded that it was only the tail, and only a little one.

While Alcott and his friends talked philosophy under the trees, his wife tried to keep the household going; little Louisa May observed: "There is only one beast of burden here—my mother."

Though Emerson agreed with the man who said that Alcott's writing "resembled a train of fifteen railroad cars with one passenger," for many years he went on helping his friend out of one scrape after another. He once set his own family to stuffing themselves with apples for the sole reason that Alcott needed money and had nothing else to sell. When the dreamer wanted to visit England for no sensible reason, Emerson meekly went to New York and delivered some special lectures to help raise the money. At one time he invited the whole Alcott tribe to come and live with him—Bronson gleefully accepted, but his wife saw what a dreadful imposition this would be, and declined.

The Sage of Concord was equally patient with another man of whom the village did not much approve. As I have recorded elsewhere in this book, Thoreau was in and out of his household for years, and looked on Emerson, only fourteen years older, as a father. His famous hut on Walden Pond was built on Emerson's land, and with his assistance.

An often-repeated story tells of the incident when Thoreau, refusing to pay taxes to a government of which he disapproved, was put into jail overnight. (He was bailed out next morning by a member of his household.) Emerson is supposed to have visited him that evening and to have said, "Why are you in there, Henry?" To which Thoreau's answer was, "Why are you *out* there, Ralph?" Meaning, of course, that all good men should refuse to pay taxes, and be jailed. Historians are skeptical of this story, for several reasons. Emerson would probably have known all about Thoreau's reasons, in advance, and the query does not sound like him, though Thoreau's rejoinder could have been made by that cross-grained individual.

A third friend in whom few others could see any possibilities was Walt Whitman. When *Leaves of Grass* was first published, almost totally ignored by critics and public, Emerson promptly wrote him: "I greet you at the beginning of a great career, which yet must have had a long foreground somewhere for such a start." Long afterward Whitman recalled: "I was simmering, simmering, simmering. Emerson brought me to boil."

In spite of the protests of his friends, who were scandalized by Whitman's frankness on sexual matters, Emerson for many years helped the poet in every way he could. He agreed with the comment that "the author of *Leaves of Grass* has every leaf but the fig leaf"; on one occasion he tramped up and down

Boston Common for hours with Walt, trying vainly to persuade him to leave out of his next book some of the franker erotic poems; but he would not break with him for this or any other reason.

Another notable crackpot in Emerson's circle was his Aunt Mary. When he was a child, and his widowed mother was struggling so hard to keep her brood alive that she had little time for any real contact with them, Aunt Mary was the strongest intellectual influence in his life. "Scorn trifles!" she told him; "The stars are nothing!"—meaning, do not be unduly impressed with anything, however remote and overwhelming. You can be anything you wish to be, she assured the boy, and the advice is echoed and reechoed in his own mature writing.

With age, Aunt Mary became more and more eccentric. Long before her death, she had sewn her own shroud and put it away in a drawer; then, her New England thrift revolting at letting good material lie idle, she made it into first a nightgown, and then a riding cape, which streamed off her shoulders as she galloped her horse over the hills. Emerson's neighbors looked askance, but he did not. In her old age (she lived to be eighty-nine) her boardinghouse keeper tried to raise the rate for room and board from a reasonable $3 a week to an outrageous $5; Aunt Mary refused either to pay it or to move out. Emerson quietly arranged to make up the difference without his aunt's knowledge.

Sometimes he could get rid of a crackpot visitor with a few unanswerable words. When a religious fanatic came to him crying that the world was about to end, he replied calmly, "Well, let it end. I think we shall do very well without it." (When the same man said the same thing to Emerson's friend, Theodore Parker, the famous clergyman answered: "That means nothing to me, Sir. I live in Boston.")

Few men can have had deeper appreciation of the beauties of sea, sky, and landscape than Emerson. Once, riding in a carriage through Yosemite Valley in 101-degree summer heat, his companions were astonished to see him hug a heavy buffalo robe about him, too transfixed with the grandeur of the scene to be conscious of the temperature. "I have a child's love [of nature]," he wrote. "I expand and live in the warm day like corn and melons."

"When I bought my farm [in Concord]," he observed, "I did not know what a bargain I had in the bluebirds, bobolinks and thrushes, which were not charged in the bill. As little did I guess what sublime mornings and sunsets I was buying, what reaches of landscape and what fields and lanes for a tramp . . . I see the spectacle of morning from the hilltop over against my house, from daybreak to sunrise, with emotion which an angel might share." Trying to make others appreciate the beauty of nature, he remarked, "If the stars should appear one night in a thousand years, how would men believe and adore and preserve for many generations the remembrance of the city of God which had been shown!" He knew that the power to see beauty in the world about us is not innate, but must be cultivated; throughout his writing runs the demand that we should seek to acquire this art. To him, it was all-important:

"Beauty, in its largest and profoundest sense, is one expression for the universe." "Truth, and goodness, and beauty, are but different phases of the same All." He noted wryly that the donkey, which is useful, is derided because it is ugly while the lion, leopard, and tiger "are allowed to tear and devour because they are handsome."

In Paris in 1848, during the abortive Revolution, he noted that the trees on the boulevards had been cut down for barricades. "At the end of a year," he observed, "we shall take account and see if the Revolution was worth the trees."

Once, walking in his garden with his wife and a friend, he saw a particularly beautiful rose. He stood silently gazing at it for some minutes and then, doffing his headgear and making a deep Elizabethan courtier's bow, "I take off my hat to it," he said.

All his life, the philosopher tried to avoid becoming entangled with any special organization or group; he felt his function was to think, and to express his thoughts so they would mean something to others. When a few friends, who shared his belief that God is everywhere, began calling themselves Transcendentalists and meeting at irregular intervals, he joined them from time to time but always grudgingly. When they went further, and set up the cooperative colony of Brook Farm, he firmly declined to become a member. He may have secretly agreed with the skeptic who observed that you could no more save a soul with a Transcendental sermon than you could get drunk on skimmed milk. Emerson refused to become editor of the Transcendental magazine, *The Dial*, until it was on its last legs, with only one hundred subscribers; in spite of heroic efforts by Thoreau, who doubled the circulation by peddling subscriptions from door to door in Concord; it gave up the ghost not long afterward.

With all his charm, Emerson, like many introverts, was incapable of loving others as demonstratively as they loved him. Bronson Alcott, who moved to Concord to be near him, once wrote of him in his *Journal*: "'Brother!' That is a kindling name. I feel the sentiment of kindred quicken within me as I write it. He is a brother of mine, and an only one. All other men seem strange to me when I think of him; for none other knows me so well and I value none so dearly."

At almost the same moment Emerson was writing in his own journal, of Alcott and his close friend Margaret Fuller: "Cold as I am, they are almost dear." At another time he wrote something perhaps more revealing than he intended: "I do with my friends as I do with my books. I would have them where I can find them, but I seldom use them." Margaret once called him "the cold stone."

The one political issue Emerson could not avoid, and did not want to, was Negro slavery. When he was twenty-three, he spent a winter in St. Augustine, Florida, for his health. Sitting in a Bible Society meeting, in a thin-walled house, he heard the auctioneer next door sell a slave mother to one owner and her four small children to another, and came back to New England raging at the indifference shared by every member of the Bible Society except himself.

When, in 1850, Congress enacted the Fugitive Slave

Law, Emerson wrote in his journal, "This filthy enactment was made in the nineteenth century by people who could read and write. I will not obey it, by God!" When his great hero, Daniel Webster, supported the law, he denounced him in a scalding phrase: "All the drops of his blood have eyes that look downward."

He deeply regretted the human weakness that makes people fail to stick to their guns when they know they are right, and he himself made a lifelong rule of speaking out, no matter what the cost, when it was needed. "When you have chosen your part," he said, "abide by it and do not weakly try to reconcile yourself with the world . . . Self-trust is the essence of heroism." He was scornful of hypocrites who "cover over their greediness with a pretended zeal for religion or patriotism and strew sugar on a bottled spider." And again: "We only use different names: He calls it attar of roses, and I call it bilge water."

Emerson was one of the earliest believers in the characteristic American philosophic system called Pragmatism; both William James and John Dewey, its chief later exponents, testified that he had expressed its central ideas when he demanded that we look outward, not inward, that we translate our thoughts into action, and that we recognize the great power of ideas in shaping the world; James called him "my beloved Master," and Dewey said he was "the one citizen of the New World fit to have his name uttered in the same breath with that of Plato."

Emerson based his philosophy on the laws of physics and chemistry. He thought that the moral universe is strictly ordered, like the physical one, and that they parallel one another. "The laws of moral nature answer to those of matter as face to face in a [looking] glass . . . The axioms of physics translate the laws of ethics . . . This relation between mind and matter is not fancied by some poet, but stands in the will of God and so is free to be known by all men."

Not only are we all children of God, but there is only one "Oversoul," residing both in God and in ourselves. Throughout the universe equality reigns, "balancing every gift and every defeat . . . Every sweet hath its sour; every evil its good." A law of compensation operates, and all evil is eventually offset by good. We have only to trust in the divine harmony, and all will be well.

From his philosophy Emerson drew a series of precepts for daily living, which constitute the greater part of all his writings and for a century have exerted a profound influence throughout the world.

Believing as he did that God's beneficent intention toward us is expressed in laws as unchanging as "two plus two equals four," Emerson felt the individual should have complete confidence in his place in the world and in his own powers. "Trust thyself," he wrote. "Every heart vibrates to that iron string . . . Nothing is at last sacred but the integrity of your own mind. . . No law can be sacred to me but that of my own nature. Self-trust is the first secret of success, the belief that if you are here the authorities of the universe put you here, and for cause, and with some task strictly appointed you in your constitution, and so long as you work at that you are well and successful."

He quoted with approval Thoreau who, anticipating Franklin Roosevelt by nearly a century, said, "Nothing is so much to be feared as fear." We should strike out boldly, dare greatly: "Hitch your wagon to a star." Use your imagination: "You could never prove to the mind of the most ingenious mollusk that such a creature as a whale were possible." Age is no impediment: "We do not count a man's years until he has nothing else to count."

He scolded his lecture audiences for being unwilling to "say noble things," waiting to read them in a book or hear someone else say them. People at heart are finer than they dare admit to each other. "Men descend to meet."

While he believed in self-confidence, he also recognized that there must be some relation between your powers and your tasks. When a callow, egotistical college boy boasted that he had written a criticism of Plato, Emerson looked at him thoughtfully and finally said, "When you strike at a King, *you must kill him.*"

Probably the most famous essay ever written by an American is Emerson's "Self Reliance," which struck a profound chord in the American spirit at the time it was written. "To believe your own thought, to believe that what is true for you in your private heart is true for all men—that is genius." "Society everywhere is in conspiracy against the manhood of every one of its members. The virtue in most requests is conformity." "Is it so bad then to be misunderstood? Pythagoras was misunderstood, and Socrates, and Jesus, and Luther, and Copernicus, and Galileo, and Newton, and every pure and wise spirit that ever took flesh. To be great is to be misunderstood." "These roses under my window make no reference to former roses or to better ones; they are for what they are; they exist with God today."

His second famous essay is "Friendship." Despite his own aloofness, no one ever saw more clearly the possible depths and heights of such a relationship; millions of people all over the world have for more than a century quoted his wise observations. "The only reward of virtue is virtue; the only way to have a friend is to be one." "A friend is a person with whom I may be sincere. Before him I may think aloud." Is friendship wasted, if its object is unworthy? "It never troubles the sun that some of his rays fall wide and vain into ungrateful space and only a small part on the reflecting planet . . . It is thought a disgrace to love unrequited. But the great will see that true love cannot be unrequited."

It was of supreme importance to Emerson that every man should both recognize the truth about himself and not try to deceive others. "A little integrity is better than any career." Indeed, he felt that to pretend to be other than what you are is almost impossible. "There is no privacy that cannot be penetrated; no secret can be kept in the civilized world. Society is a masked ball, where everyone hides his real character, and reveals it by hiding." The truth is, "manners impress as they indicate real power; a man inspires affection and honor because he was not lying in wait for them."

The philosopher was sad to see "simplicity of character and the sovereignty of ideas broken up by the prevalence of secondary desires—the desire of riches, of pleasure, of power and of praise." To him this was "employing a paper currency when there is no bullion in the vault." Emerson, who in his whole life never once made any pretense of being something he was not, summed it up: "Hell is better than Heaven, if the man in Hell knows his place, and the man in Heaven does not."

His belief that moral laws are as unchanging as those of physics or chemistry made him also believe that we must accept, and trust in, the natural order, as the basis for success and happiness. "A healthy soul stands united with the just and the true as a magnet arranges itself with the pole. God is positive," he explained. "Evil is merely privative [the absence of something], not absolute: It is like cold which is the privation [lack] of heat. All evil is so much death or nonentity." Once you have "accepted your own law, all omens are good, all stars officious [helpful], all men your allies, all parts of life take order and beauty." It is actions that count. "Don't *say* things. What you are stands over you the while and thunders so that I cannot hear what you say to the contrary." Yet he recognized that "greatness in a man is often hidden until it is needed, and in fact, a great individual is more important than the sum of his deeds . . . Character [is] a reserve force which acts directly by presence and without means."

Each of us has his own secret talent and must find it. "Do your work! I have to say this often but Nature says it oftener." We should let other people alone, to be themselves, and enjoy life in their own way. "You are trying to make that man another *you*. One's enough!"

"Great men," said Emerson, "are they who see that

the spiritual is stronger than any material force; that thoughts rule the world." This is because of the Oversoul. "When it breathes through the intellect it is genius; when it breathes through the will it is virtue; when it flows through the affection it is love!" Spelling this out, he explained: "There is one soul. It is related to the world. Art is its action thereon. Science finds its methods. Literature is its record. Religion is the emotion of reverence that it inspires. Ethics is the soul illustrated in human life. Society is the finding of this soul by individuals in each other."

The most familiar of all Emerson's sayings has been badly mangled in the public memory. It is usually given as, "If a man build a better mousetrap than his neighbor, though he build his house in the woods the world will make a beaten path to his door." This version was publicized by Elbert Hubbard; it is actually a truncated form of something Mrs. Sarah Yule claimed she had heard Emerson say in a lecture, which she printed in a book called *Borrowings*, of which Mary S. Keene was coauthor. What Emerson really wrote in his journal was a little more sensible: "I trust a good deal to common fame, as we all must. If a man has good corn, or wood, or boards, or pigs, to sell, or can make better chairs or knives, crucibles or church organs, than anybody else, you will find a broad, hard-beaten road to his house, though it be in the woods."

Fashions change in poetry even more rapidly than in prose, and for that reason, Emerson's essays are more read today than his verse, with a few exceptions that I have already noted. His Transcendentalism is expressed in one poem that is still well known, "Brahma," with its enigmatic first stanza:

> If the red slayer thinks he slays
> Or if the slain think he is slain,
> They know not well the subtle ways
> I keep, and pass, and turn again.

Emerson's optimistic, affirmative philosophy found strong expression in his belief that most men underrate themselves. "If a single man plant himself indomitably on his instinct," he said, in his Phi Beta Kappa speech in 1837, "and there abide, the huge world will come round to him." One of his biographers, Phillips Russell, remarks that this single sentence has dominated American thought ever since. "In all my lectures I have taught one doctrine," Emerson said, "namely, the infinitude of the private man . . . The good mind chooses what is positive, what is advancing—embraces the affirmative . . . Don't be a cynic and disconsolate creature. Don't bewail and bemoan." And he added: "The affirmative of affirmatives is love."

He believed in a healthy recognition of your own value to the world. "No man can do anything well who does not esteem his work to be of importance . . . All the thoughts of a turtle are turtle . . . What is a weed? A plant whose virtues have not yet been discovered."

He recognized, to be sure, that people vary in their capabilities: "We boil at different degrees." We also develop at varying rates. "I went by him in the night.

Who can tell the moment when the pine outgrew the whortleberry that shaded its first sprout? It went by in the night."

In his day as now, there were intellectual snobs. When he heard one such say that "the sermon was good for you and me but not understood by the great mass," he wrote in his journal: "Don't you deceive yourself, say I. The great mass understands what's what as well as the little mass."

Because he believed in a beneficent universe, Emerson summoned his followers to take risks, defy the views of those about them, to live dangerously if danger meant reality and truth. The three qualities "which conspicuously attract the wonder and reverence of mankind" are disinterestedness, power, and courage. Courage does not mean the absence of fear, but overcoming it; it is being equal to your problem. "They can conquer who believe they can. It is he who has done the deed once who does not shrink from attempting it again." "What have I gained," he asks, "if I quake at public opinion, or at the threat of assault? If I quake, what matters it what I quake at?" This includes the fear of death. "Don't tell me to get ready to die. The only preparation I can make is by fulfilling my present duties."

In 1837 at the age of thirty-four, Emerson made himself famous with a single speech, his Phi Beta Kappa oration at Harvard, in which he urged American scholars not to cling to the past, or to Europe, but to stand on their own feet and make their own judgments. His words clanged across the country like a fire alarm. At a time when education consisted chiefly of getting the classics practically by heart, he demanded that young men should spend their time thinking, not reading. "The centuries," he said, "are conspirators against the sanity and authority of the soul . . . Books are but crutches, the resorts of the feeble and lame, which, if used by the strong, weaken the muscular power and become necessary aids." Even the classics can be wrong: "A popgun is a popgun, though the ancient and the honorable of the earth insist it is the crack of doom."

To be sure, we should know what has been said before us. "The past has baked my loaf, and in the strength of its bread I break up the old oven." "Meek young men," he remarked, "grow up in libraries, believing it their duty to accept the views which Cicero, which Locke, which Bacon, have given; forgetful that Cicero, Locke, and Bacon were only young men in libraries when they wrote these books." He challenged his hearers with a stirring call: "We will walk on our own feet; we will work with our own hands; we will speak our own minds." These words, said Oliver Wendell Holmes, Sr., were "America's intellectual Declaration of Independence."

All his life Emerson fought the disease so prevalent in America today, the greed for possessions. "Things are in the saddle, and ride mankind," he observed. "Why should you renounce your right to traverse the star-lit deserts of truth for the premature comforts of an acre, house and barn? . . . Make yourself necessary to the world and mankind will give you bread . . . Riches and poverty are a thick or thin costume; and our life—the life of all of us—identical."

He was delighted when his friend, Louis Agassiz, asked to do something for remuneration, answered indignantly, "I can't waste my time in earning money." A favorite story was that of the English doctor in India who, bothered by a patient when he was dissecting a tiger, demanded: "Do you think I can leave my work for your damned guinea?" Describing what he saw about him in America, Emerson wrote: "We are paralyzed with fear; we hold onto our little properties, house and land, office and money, for the bread which they have in our experience yielded us, although we confess that our being does not flow through them."

Here again, he practiced what he preached. When at thirty-two he decided thenceforth to do nothing but write or lecture, he knew he was taking a perpetual vow of poverty, but never in fifty years did he swerve from that course. At a time when he needed money badly the Salem Lyceum offered him a good fee to lecture, "provided no allusions are made to religious controversy or other exciting topics upon which the public mind is honestly divided." He replied the same day, quoting these words, and saying, "I am really sorry that any person in Salem should think me capable of accepting an invitation so encumbered."

Emerson enjoyed intensely every moment of life; as he says repeatedly, the beauty of nature in all her aspects was almost too poignant to bear. One of his biographers, the late F. O. Matthiessen, observes that "the first and recurrent upsurge of his conviction was that 'life is an ecstasy,' that the moment was an almost unbelievable miracle which he wanted, more than anything else, to catch and record." His attitude was the direct opposite of, and a reaction from, the grim-faced, dour Calvinism that had dominated New England for two hundred years.

Even when things were at their worst, after the death of one he loved, or in any other adversity, he never wavered in his belief that to be alive is a joy. The key word *ecstasy* recurs constantly in his writing; he referred to the lecture platform as the place for "ecstasy and eloquence," and defined genius as "that excess of life which we call ecstasy." "I embrace absolute life," he said, meaning the sour as well as the sweet, the incomprehensible as well as that which is made plain. His optimism seemed to some of his contemporaries excessive, but he could never have laid the magic of his healing touch on so many millions without it.

Emerson lived long before Freud had made "the unconscious mind" a household phrase; but he seemed to sense intuitively the heart of the doctrine. "Blessed is the child," he wrote. "The Unconscious is ever the act of God himself." "Nobody can reflect upon an unconscious act with regret or contempt. Our spontaneous action is always the best." "A man finds out that there is [something] in him that knows more than he does." If you will but trust this inner man you cannot fail. Within or beyond your individual life there is "a universal soul wherein as in a firmament the natures of Justice, Truth, Love, Freedom, arise and shine." Over and over he emphasized that "sin is when a man is untrue to his own constitution."

Emerson felt that "intuition is an outwelling from

the universal mind . . . [which is] the sole creator of both the useful and the beautiful . . . [Therefore] the only way for the individual to partake in the creative act is by submitting himself entirely to this primal source [that is] beyond the understanding."

Many years before Theodore Roosevelt talked of "the strenuous life," Emerson was preaching—and practicing—the same doctrine. In spite of his frail health, he drove himself remorselessly. Far into old age he could be found every winter traveling thousands of miles by whatever means were available to fill his lecture engagements, speaking night after night in drafty halls that were always too hot or too cold, and then racing on, in fair weather or foul, to his next town. When at home, he shut himself up for long hours each day in his study, where he produced not only his ten major books and scores of magazine articles and lectures, but the million words and more of his journal.

He accepted the idea that the more you give to the world, the richer you are, and illustrated it by observing that the more ideas he expressed, the more he seemed to have. "Like the New England soil," he observed, "my talent is good only whilst I work it . . . [Artists], like bees, must put their lives into the sting they give. What is man good for without enthusiasm? . . . He who has put forth his total strength in fit actions has the richest return." Too much soft life is bad for you: "The hard soil and four months of snow make the inhabitant of the Northern Temperate Zone wiser and abler than his fellow who enjoys the fixed smile of the tropics."

It is not enough merely to be a thinker: "An action is the perfection and publication of thought."

His lectures, which always took exactly one hour to deliver, were preceded by a minimum of twenty hours of preparation, and when he was dissatisfied, he doubled or trebled the amount. "The sum of wisdom," he wrote, "is that the time is never lost that is devoted to work."

In spite of his affection for Thoreau, he found the naturalist disappointingly relaxed. "Thoreau [lacks] a little ambition in his mixture. [Because] of this, instead of being the head of American Engineers he is captain of the Huckleberry Party."

Constantly urging people to try the difficult, he told them: "Do not be too timid and squeamish about your actions . . . What if you do fail and get fairly rolled in the dirt once or twice? Up again, you shall never be so afraid of a tumble . . . Calamities are our friends. Try the rough water as well as the smooth; rough water can teach lessons worth knowing . . . Difficulties exist to be surmounted. The great heart would no more complain of the obstruction that makes success hard than of the iron wall of the gun which hinders the shot from scattering."

Toward the end of his life, Emerson's magnificent mind began to give way. Like many another, he forgot names. Groping for the word *umbrella,* he described the object: "People take them away." Attending the funeral of Longfellow in the year of his own death, 1882, he gazed into the coffin, and afterward said, "That gentleman was a sweet, beautiful soul, but I have forgotten his name."

Five years earlier, he had been one of the men at the dinner William Dean Howells gave in celebration of the seventieth birthday of Whittier, at which Mark Twain suffered the worst humiliation of his life. Mark, impressed by the distinguished company of Boston Brahmins he was to face, had written out a speech on what seemed to him a funny theme—the misadventures of three old tramps named Henry Wadsworth Longfellow, Oliver Wendell Holmes, and Ralph Waldo Emerson. Reporting the deeds of these old scamps, he wove into the dialogue actual quotations from the writings of the three men. Today this seems a harmless notion, but for some reason, nobody at the dinner laughed as Mark ploughed on, increasingly desperate in the awful chill. The Bostonians were of course unforgivably rude to their guest, whatever they thought of his performance. Mark believed his life was ruined; he wrote abject letters of apology to all concerned.

But it turned out that Emerson, who sat stony-faced like the others, hadn't heard a word of it. His hearing was excellent, but his thoughts were far away. Next day his wife read the skit to him, and he reported that it had amused him.

He was the outstanding personality among all the famous men at that dinner table; it is interesting to speculate that perhaps the others watched for him to smile, ready to do the same or go even further.

Emerson died April 27, 1882, mourned by all the world.

Today, so many years after his death, some of his ideas have of course suffered the inevitable erosion of time; but his chief contributions are just as valuable today as when they first thrilled his readers. Above all, he teaches us that personality, sacred and inviolable, is the most important thing in the world. It is the lesson humanity needs above all others today.

six

Henry David Thoreau: Rebel with a Cause

RARELY IN all history has a man been so poorly regarded by his contemporaries as Thoreau, only to have his reputation still growing a hundred years after his death. Hardly anybody took him seriously while he was still alive. To the worthy burghers of Concord he was that lazy young Thoreau, who barely earned his living, part of the time, as surveyor, pencil maker, or Ralph Waldo Emerson's handyman. He was chiefly recalled as "the man who once [accidentally] set fire to the woods and burned a hundred acres of good timber."

The professor of English at Harvard under whom he studied said there was only one promising writer in his class—and named somebody else, a man whose total works consisted of one book for children, who is now forgotten.

Thoreau's great work, *Walden,* was ignored by most contemporary writers; some thought it must be a parody or hoax. It sold only one edition of two thousand copies during his lifetime; this was better than the only other book published during his lifetime, *A Week on the Concord and Merrimack Rivers,* of which only 206 copies were bought. The publisher returned the unsold copies to him, and he wrote in his journal, "I now possess a library of nine hundred volumes, more than seven hundred of which I wrote myself." He would be surprised if he could know that a copy of this edition of the book, published at $1.25, is worth $600 today, and one with his name signed on the flyleaf is valued at $1,000. A single sheet of his six-thousand-page handwritten journal finds a ready sale at $250.

Walden has probably been translated into more languages than any other American book; it sells every year scores of times as many copies as during the author's whole life. Scholars say that published references to and quotations from him grow more numerous every day. Thousands of people quote, without knowing the source, his famous statement,

"The mass of men lead lives of quiet desperation," or chuckle over his shrewd observation, "Some circumstantial evidence is very strong, as when you find a trout in the milk."

For a hundred years after his death, Thoreau, who fought so hard against the "bitch goddess, Success," who wanted men to live by the spirit and not by physical things, seemed a voice crying in the wilderness. But then in the 1960s and 1970s, a new generation of young people appeared, who became disciples of the Concord seer. To the dismay of their elders, they repudiated material success as a proper goal for mankind, sought to return as far as possible to Nature's ways, tried to understand themselves and each other, preferred love to hate, sought cooperation, not competition. Perhaps the pendulum will again swing the other way, but for the present Thoreau is winning to a degree nobody in his day, or for a century after, would have believed possible.

Thoreau (who had been christened David Henry, but changed the order of his names for the sake of euphony), spent almost his whole life within a mile or two of the spot in Concord, Massachusetts, where he was born. When he was a year old his family moved a few miles away, but they came back before he was six. He was four years at Harvard and a few months on Staten Island working as a tutor; he visited Canada and in the last year of his life he went briefly as a tourist to Minnesota. Otherwise he never strayed from the little stretch of earth he knew so well and made so famous. He worked intermittently in the family pencil factory, and as noted, did odd jobs of surveying, and was a handyman for Ralph Waldo Emerson and others. Since his poverty was largely a matter of choice, he professed not to mind it and insisted that he was happier than most men.

Thoreau's health was always frail; he had "weak lungs," and his premature death at forty-five was hastened when he insisted on keeping a lecture engagement in stormy weather, though he already had a cold.

Fresh out of Harvard, he was hired to teach the village one-room school, but at once, disturbing rumors about him began to circulate. It was said that he did not whip the children—and everyone knew that you could not run a school properly without liberal use of the rod.

When this abnormal state of affairs had continued for about two weeks, a member of the school board visited the young pedagogue in the classroom and laid down an ultimatum. He must resort to the birch, or lose his post. The town could not afford to have its young people ruined by the eccentric ideas of a young crank.

The teacher was equal to the occasion. Before the day was out, he called up six pupils selected at random and administered the required corporal punishment (or a reasonable facsimile). Then he went home and wrote a curt letter of resignation. He would teach no more in any school that demanded brutality which is so obviously unnecessary if a teacher knows his business.

Many millions of people, around the world, have been deeply influenced by Thoreau's magnificently phrased exhortations that we must always subordinate material success to spiritual progress, defy authority when it is in the wrong, be our own judges of our conduct.

His essay on civil disobedience was a textbook for Gandhi in India, as it has been for American Negroes resisting segregation. They have learned from him the lesson of passive protest. Don't fight force with force, he said; register your opposition to injustice by refusal to cooperate, nothing more and nothing less. Go into this policy with your eyes open, knowing that it requires the highest possible level of moral courage. Be prepared to go to prison, to be cursed, beaten, and starved. Repay hate with love, and above all, stick to your principles.

The central theme of Thoreau's philosophy is his insistence on the absolute freedom of the individual—freedom, not license, for he proposed that every man should lay heavy burdens of conscience on himself. He felt that we can only be true to ourselves when we are not pushed out of our destined course by pressure from possessions, people, public opinion, government.

No one can be certain of the origin of the ideas that Thoreau expounded throughout his life from the age of twenty. There may be a clue in the fact that he grew up in a poor family, looked down upon by a narrow, even bigoted small town, in which he could see all too clearly how conformity was forced upon the prosperous by their very prosperity.

Thoreau was a man financially poor but rich with personal intellectual resources. "I have never found a companion," he remarked, "that was so companionable as solitude. I would rather sit on a pumpkin and have it all to myself than be crowded on a velvet cushion." As a young man he tried to buy a farm on the installment plan, in order to live a solitary life; he offered the farmer a down payment of $10, which is all he had. The farmer was agreeable but his wife said no.

Then at age twenty-eight he borrowed land from Ralph Waldo Emerson on the shore of Walden Pond, and built with his own hands a hut whose materials cost him $28—and built it so well that a hundred years later the walls were still in use, as a private garage in Concord. In this hut he lived for two years, recording in a journal what he did and thought. Nine years later, when he was thirty-seven, he published the rewritten and amplified contents of his journal in the book, *Walden*, that has swept around the world.

All his writings appeared first in his journal and were then worked over into final form, so that his thoughts leap out at you like minerals under ultraviolet light. No American author can be studied to better effect by the beginning writer. In his journal he recorded not only the profound ideas of his philosophy, but everyday incidents: the heroic efforts of a dozen people to recapture an escaped pig; a storekeeper who, lacking small change, made up for it by giving the customer pins, stuck into his coat lapel; a swimmer so powerful that he swam a river with a jug in each hand; the beauty of lamplight shining through a snowbank from a hollowed-out aperture. He felt that all writers should put down their thoughts as fast as possible, and then review at leisure. "Write while the heat is in you. The writer who postpones the recording of his thoughts uses an iron which has cooled, to burn a hole with."

Why does Thoreau appeal so tremendously today? It is because the evils he fought are so much more apparent today than they were a hundred years ago.

He urged that honest men should refuse to do the bidding of a wicked government; few governments are as wicked as the totalitarian dictatorships of our time.

He wanted people to be free of the pressure of material things; that pressure has grown with the years.

He emphasized, always and everywhere, the need to be in harmony with Nature and Nature's laws; as life grows increasingly artificial and complicated, the wisdom of his advice becomes more and more apparent.

He drank in eagerly the beauty of natural things, sunrise and sunset, snowstorm or June morning; we need to remember his passion in a time when the wilderness is rapidly being overrun by our exploding population which has pushed its concrete fingers of roadway everywhere and torn out lovely old orchards to make room for suburban tracts.

And perhaps most of all, we need his doctrine of love for your fellow man, in a day when the world seems dedicated to hatred and mass destruction.

Most people have heard four things about Thoreau, all of them wrong.

First, he was not austere and unapproachable. He

sometimes seemed so to strangers, but most of those who knew him well found him cordial and sympathetic. He got on particularly well with the poor immigrants who lived in his neighborhood, many of whom consulted him whenever they needed advice. Louisa May Alcott, a good judge of character, reported how he "used to come smiling up to his neighbors, to announce that the bluebirds had arrived, with as much interest in the fact as other men take in messages by the Atlantic cable."

Second, he was not a women hater. Twice in his life he was deeply in love, but tragic circumstances in both cases prevented marriage.

Third, he was not a simple, self-taught child of Nature. He was graduated from Harvard in the top tenth of his class, at a time when college students worked very hard indeed. He was well grounded in all the classics, read Latin and Greek fluently, spoke French, German, Italian, and a little Spanish.

It is true, however, that he was not a highly trained naturalist. Since his study of Nature was haphazard and spontaneous, there were sometimes surprising gaps in his knowledge. He scorned the professional scientists of his day who spent most of their time listing and classifying things. "It is not worth the while to go round the world to count the cats in Zanzibar." But he was no mere gifted amateur. He caught bees in a box, dusted their wings with powder of different colors, and then released them. He was thus able to find which bees went where, and he also checked the duration of their flights to chosen flowers. He knew eight hundred of the twelve hundred plants now known in the area of Concord, and made a collection of about eight hundred Indian artifacts.

Fourth, he did not live solitary, far from civilization. His hut in the woods, described in *Walden*, was only a mile or so from the village of Concord, and he could and occasionally did walk home for a meal with his parents.

While he was self-taught as a naturalist, he disciplined himself rigidly when he wanted to know something. One spring, he wished to find the exact date on which a certain flower would bloom, and the nearest specimen was five miles away. For ten days he walked that ten-mile round trip. On the tenth day, the flower had bloomed, and he recorded the date in his journal. Emerson marveled at his seemingly supernatural knowledge of what went on in the pastures and forests.

A farmer once told Mrs. Daniel Chester French, wife of the famous American sculptor, that he had seen Thoreau standing and looking at a pond in the morning. He was still there at noon, and at night. Finally the farmer asked him what he was doing, and reported that he said, "Mr. Murray, I'm a-studyin'—the habits—of the bullfrog!"

Thoreau's lifelong love affair with the out-of-doors is celebrated in words that sing their way into our hearts. "For many years I was self-appointed inspector of snowstorms and rainstorms, and did my duty faithfully. I have spent a couple of years with the flowers chiefly, having none other so binding engagement as to observe when they open. It is true, I never assisted the sun materially in his rising; but doubt not, it was of the last importance to be present at it." He took a walk in the woods every afternoon, he explained, "to see what I have caught in my traps which I set for facts." Nobody has bettered his words about the snowflake with its endlessly varied six sides: "A divinity must have stirred within them before the crystals did thus shoot and set . . . these glorious spangles, the sweepings of heaven's floor. And they all sing, melting as they sing, of the mysteries of the number—six, six, six."

Some of his descriptions have become famous, like his word-pictures of chasing a fox in the snow, studying a woodchuck at a distance of only a few feet, a battle between red and black ants, or paddling after a loon across the placid surface of a lake.

He had a wonderful way with the native animals and birds of the area. Frederick Willis quotes a report on how they came to him when he signaled.

> He gave a low, curious whistle; immediately a woodchuck came running toward him from a nearby burrow. With varying note, yet still low and strange, a pair of gray squirrels were summoned, and approached him fearlessly. With still another note, several birds, including two crows, flew toward him, one of the crows nestling upon his shoulder . . . He fed them all from his hand, taking food from his pocket, and petted them gently before our delighted gaze; and then dismissed them by different whistling, always strange and low and short, each little wild thing departing instantly at hearing its special signal.

This story comes at second hand from Bronson Alcott. Even if he exaggerated a little in his enthusiasm, the residue is still impressive.

Thoreau was one of the earliest American conservationists. He suffered when he saw a beautiful tree being cut down—and described it in unforgettable prose. He deplored the new dams which prevented the shad from completing their life cycle by journeying upstream to where they had been spawned. He even grumbled publicly when an enterprising businessman cut a lot of ice on Walden Pond; the ice proved unsalable and a great lump of it sat awhile on the shore.

Always he wanted things to be done as simply and naturally as possible. When he was still a student, he protested because his father bought maple sugar instead of letting him make it. "He said it took me from my studies. I said I made it my study; I felt as if I had been to a university."

Quite early in his life, Thoreau gave up shooting wild animals, and he even fished with increasing reluctance. Asked to kill a turtle for the zoological museum at Harvard, he reported that he felt he had had "a murderer's experience to a degree." He was furious with the chicken raisers of Concord who shot hawks. "I would rather never taste chickens' meat nor hens' eggs than never to see a hawk sailing through the upper air again."

Thoreau was far from handsome in any conventional sense. He was only five feet, seven inches tall, with limbs too short for his trunk. He had large, frank, gray-blue eyes, thick brown hair, often in disarray, sloping shoulders, and a narrow chest. Nathaniel Hawthorne remarked that he was "as ugly as sin, long nose, queer mouth . . . but his ugliness is of an honest and agreeable fashion, and becomes him much better than beauty."

Though some people thought him lacking in social graces, many found pleasure in his company. He could play the flute, and was fond of doing so. Children loved him; he did simple sleight-of-hand tricks for them, including quartering an apple and making it seem whole again by sticking the parts back together. He told them stories, and fashioned whistles and even little flutes, from reeds.

Like most other New Englanders of his generation, Thoreau could do almost anything that needed doing; he was carpenter, plasterer, stonemason, bricklayer. Emerson, almost helpless at these simple tasks, marveled at him and he in turn chuckled at that unworldly philosopher who once, seeing his own calf loose in his own yard, did not recognize it, opened the gate, and drove it away.

Thoreau had the shrewd New England common sense that Emerson sometimes lacked. Living in Concord, he wanted to draw books from the Harvard Library but was refused on the ground that Concord was too far away. Not at all, he retorted; the railroad having been built, Concord was now nearer to Cambridge than Boston was in stagecoach days. He won his point.

Thoreau was adept in the use of small boats; his first book, *A Week on the Concord and Merrimack Rivers*, describes a voyage he and his brother John undertook in a boat Henry had built. He was such a skilled woodsman that he could walk through the thick forest around Walden Pond in the blackest night, feeling a faint path with his feet and identifying familiar individual trees by touching them as he passed.

He was a good skater. Rose Hawthorne, Nathaniel's daughter, wrote a wonderful description of a scene many people today would give a fortune to have witnessed, when Emerson, Hawthorne, and Thoreau went skating together. Hawthorne, "wrapped in his cloak, moved like a self-impelled Greek statue, stately and grave." Emerson, "evidently too weary to hold himself erect, pitched head foremost, half lying on the air." Thoreau on the other hand did "dithyrambic dances and Bacchic leaps on the ice."

Though he loved solitude, he also sometimes loved company. Living by Walden Pond, he would set a chair outside the door as a signal to his friends that they were now welcome. To be sure, some of them stayed too long, and he mentioned in his journal those "who did not know when their visit had terminated, though I went about my business again, answering them from greater and greater remoteness." When he was out of earshot, even the dullest could take the hint.

Few men ever lived in whom doctrine and action were so perfectly combined. Thoreau urged people to conquer "the tyranny of things," and went through life with a minimum of useless baggage. When he lived in his $28 hut, his food (in addition to what he raised or found growing wild in the woods) cost him only twenty-seven cents a week. He boasted that by omitting all nonessentials, he could support himself for a year by doing only six weeks' labor, and thought this was a fine way to live. He once mused in his journal at some length on the possibility of residing in a big toolbox such as were used by the railroad construction gangs. "Every man who was hard pushed might get such a one for a dollar, and having bored a few auger holes in it, to admit the air at least, get into it when it rains and at night, and hook down the lid . . . and in his soul be free. Many a man is harassed to death to pay the rent of a larger and more luxurious box who would not have frozen to death in such a box as this."

Even during the years when he worked more than usual, managing the family business of manufacturing pencils, he firmly refused to toil all day. His afternoons were kept for a three-hour walk in the woods and meadows around Concord. He complained about visitors who refused to walk with him, and who spoiled his afternoons by wanting to sit indoors and talk or to have a nap.

Sometimes he took longer trips, on foot, sleeping on the ground at night, carrying "a dipper, a spoon, a fish line, some Indian meal, salt and sugar." He caught fish and cooked them, or bought bread and milk at a farmhouse. "I have traveled thus," he recorded, "some hundreds of miles without taking any meal in a house, sleeping on the ground when convenient, and found it cheaper and in many respects more profitable than staying at home."

On his walks, whether long or short, he always

carried an umbrella, thus avoiding, as he said, the need for a raincoat. He had a homemade knapsack, a notebook, and an old volume for pressing flowers. On long trips, he also carried a bundle tied up in a handkerchief or wrapped in paper, containing the things mentioned above and a change of linen. Invariably he came home with his pockets (and often his hat as well) overflowing with specimens—flowers, bits of rock, all sorts of oddments. When his notebook was full, or he had forgotten to carry it, he made a passable substitute from a piece of birch bark.

Thoreau's father had failed as a storekeeper before setting up the pencil factory, which never earned very much, though it finally developed a fairly profitable sideline in selling graphite to the just-invented electroplating industry. The son had to have a scholarship to get through Harvard, and worked hard during his vacations. The college relaxed for his benefit a rigid rule that every student must wear a black coat to the daily chapel; Thoreau had only one and it was green. He was too poor to pay $5 for his sheepskin, which gave rise to the false report, still circulated, that for some reason he had refused to accept his degree. But he was never a fanatic alumnus. When Emerson once boasted that Harvard taught most of the branches of learning, Thoreau answered, "Yes, indeed, all the branches and none of the roots."

Some years after he was graduated he contributed $5 to a fund to buy books for impoverished students and remarked, "This is more than I have earned in the last three months." When money was being raised to help out Bronson Alcott, Emerson gave $100,

Longfellow and Lowell gave $50 each, but Thoreau unblushingly gave $1, the amount he felt was appropriate to the state of his exchequer.

Since his poverty was voluntary, he resented anyone's patronizing or condoling with him about it. A few years out of college he reported on himself for the annual class record, saying, "I am a schoolmaster, a private tutor, a surveyor, a gardener, a farmer, a painter (I mean a house painter), a carpenter, a mason, a day laborer, a pencil maker . . . a writer and sometimes a poetaster [poet]." He added, "I have found out a way to live without what is commonly called employment or industry, attractive or otherwise." But he went on to say, "I beg that the class [of 1837] will not consider me an object of charity, and if any of them are in want of any pecuniary assistance, and will make known their case to me, I will engage to give them some advice of more worth than money."

Though he sometimes pretended to a general pessimism, he really shared the hopefulness of his era, when America was expanding hugely and just beginning to tap the vast resources of the West. "We look to windward for fair weather," he said in his cryptic way, meaning that no matter how bad the past may be, we feel sure the future will be better.

When Thoreau told people to defy the wicked orders of a wicked government, he was not preaching what he feared to practice. As noted, he went to jail rather than pay a trifling poll tax to a state that condoned human slavery; he would have stayed there had not a member of his household, against his will, paid the tax and let him out. After John Brown's raid, when the old man was about to be hanged, and the sentiment of the country seemed heavily against him, Thoreau fearlessly delivered a stirring oration in his defense.

Emerson was a little slow in speaking out for the abolition of slavery, but finally agreed to do so. Thoreau went from door to door in Concord, asking people to come to the meeting in the courthouse. The town bell was in the steeple of the First Parish Church, but the sexton, apparently on political grounds, refused to ring it to signal the meeting; Thoreau rang it himself.

He had firsthand contact with the terrible results of slavery. As a boy, he knew of an old Negro in Concord who had actually been kidnapped in Africa, and sometimes wept for his lost wife and children. As a man, Thoreau befriended an escaped slave, the illegitimate son of a white man in Virginia, who was negotiating to buy his freedom from his own father; the latter cold-bloodedly set a price of $600, more than the son could pay. The writer-naturalist was angered by a fellow townsman in Concord, who had answered an appeal by a free Negro woman to help her buy her husband out of slavery in the South. The Concord man bought the husband for $600 and then demanded $800 of the wife.

Thoreau ran real risks in breaking the law by helping fugitive slaves escape to Canada; Concord was on the Underground Railroad. He kept fugitives in his house overnight, and drove them to a railroad station some distance away where they had a good chance of slipping on board the train undetected. It is not surprising that he wrote, "I cannot for an instant recognize that political organization as *my* government which is the *slave's* government also."

It was part of his acceptance of mankind as fundamentally good that he should continue to trust people even when his confidence was abused. There was no lock on the door of his hut at Walden, even though he sometimes left it for several weeks. Only two things were stolen; one of them was a volume of Homer, and the other was a dipper that two young women borrowed to go and get a drink from the lake. The loss of the Homer he took philosophically, but the theft of the dipper annoyed him, since he had seen the miscreants face to face. "They were a disgrace to their sex and to humanity," he recorded severely.

There seems no doubt, from certain cryptic references in his journal, that young Thoreau was at one time deeply in love with the wife of one of his best friends, perhaps Mrs. Emerson. We can assume, from his sensitive code of ethics, that he never gave her, or anyone else, any indication of his feelings.

His other love affair was equally tragic. As a youth of twenty he met and fell in love with a young woman, and was on the brink of proposing to her when he discovered that his older brother, John, whom he had idolized all his life, was in love with the same girl. Henry promptly sealed his lips, giving neither John nor the girl (Miss Ellen Sewall) any hint of his feeling. John proposed and was accepted, but Miss Sewall's father immediately forced her to break the engagement.

Not long after, John, in fragile health for years,

died without warning. His hands now freed, Henry in turn proposed and was accepted; but once more Mr. Sewall forced his daughter to break the engagement to a young man who, in the father's eyes, was a ne'er-do-well who would certainly never amount to anything. When Henry was near death, someone mentioned Ellen's name in his presence, and, astonishingly for him, he murmured, "I have always loved her," repeating a moment later, "I have always loved her."

What are the things Thoreau has to say to us today that are of such importance that he is heard around the world? He demanded of others, as he did of himself, that they should never be satisfied with the applause of the crowd if they knew they were capable of doing better. "If one advances confidently in the direction of his dreams," he wrote, "and endeavors to live the life which he has imagined," he will deserve his own respect. Expediency is never right. "If I have unjustly wrested a plank from a drowning man, I must restore it to him though I drown myself."

You must dare to be different and tolerate differences in others. "If a man does not keep pace with his companions, perhaps it is because he hears a different drummer. Let him step to the music which he hears, however measured or far away." He abhorred coercion. "I was not born to be forced. I will breathe after my own fashion."

All his life Thoreau both preached and practiced the necessity of doing now what you most want to do, what is most important for you. To young people who wanted to become writers but procrastinated he had only one sentence of advice: Go up into the garret and write. Sometimes he sounds as though he had a premonition of the shortness of his own life. He argued seriously that if you want to take a trip it is better to start out on foot *now*, rather than wait to work, save money, and buy a train ticket. He predicted to a friend that by following the first course he would beat him to their common destination.

He was impatient of those who spent so much time studying life that they never start to live. "It is only when we forget all our learning that we begin to know." You must not only live, but live to the full. "Why do we not let on the flood, raise the gates, and set all our wheels in motion? With most men life is postponed to some trivial business and so therefore is Heaven."

You must enjoy as you go along, and this is only possible when you perform your tasks without undue sense of strain. The best work is accompanied "by a wide halo of ease and leisure. Why should the hen set all day? She can lay but one egg, and besides, she will not have picked up materials for a new one." It is safe to say that by following his own doctrine Thoreau got more happiness out of his forty-five years than do many men out of eighty. It was inconceivable to him that any man should want to do less than his best at every moment of his life. He got his pleasure from the contemplation of beauty, from making himself one with Nature, from knowing that as far as was within him he had cast out those twin devils, fear and pride.

While Thoreau urged us to break every crippling bond of conventional opinion, of things, money, fame, "respectability," he did not condone irresponsibility. He had the idea, echoed by some existentialists today, that each of us is involved in everything that happens. "Our least deed, like the young of the land crab, wends its way to the sea of cause and effect as soon as born and makes a drop there to eternity."

No one should excuse himself by saying that things are out of control, and too strong for him. "All fear of the world or consequences is swallowed up in a manly anxiety to do Truth justice." If there is evil, you must not participate but must oppose it, no matter what the consequences to yourself; you must not make excuses by saying you were merely following orders. "We all do stand in the front ranks of the battle every moment of our lives; where there is a brave man, there is the thickest of the fight, there the post of honor."

When Thoreau tells us to "simplify, simplify!" he is not joking. If you would play your part in the world you must strip for action. Possessions are like leg-irons. He kept his belongings at such a minimum that during his two years at Walden he could set all the furniture of his hut out on the grass within a few minutes—where, he observed, it suited the landscape so well that he could hardly bear to put it back.

We must get rid of ideas as well as things. Don't clutter your mind with useless information; sweep out the old, discarded ideas daily, just as you sweep the dust from the floor. There is little enough room in your mind even for the great thoughts. "By poverty—i.e., simplicity of life, fewness of incidents, I am solidified and crystallized. It is a singular concentration of strength and energy and flavor." You should come as fresh and pure to your daily communion with Nature as the pine tree on the mountainside lifting its head to Heaven.

He once summed up his position in the world, in a letter to a friend, Harrison Blake: "I have no designs on society—or nature—or God. I am simply what I am, or I begin to be that. I *live* in the *present*. I only remember the past—and anticipate the future."

You must fight and fight hard, all your life, he tells us, to maintain your independence. There is a conspiracy of society, parents, school, to make you conform: Resist it! Take no man's ideas for granted—not even Thoreau's—without checking them for yourself. The philosophers of ancient times were not necessarily wise merely because they were ancient. There is no such thing as a "position of authority" that is automatically right; every position of authority must be earned afresh every day by uttering demonstrable truth.

We give hostages to fortune if we first decide what standard of living we must have and then try to see how we can earn that much money. The process should be reversed: Decide first how much time you care to give to earning your living and set your standard of life accordingly. Before you try to keep up with the Joneses you should first find out where the Joneses are going and whether that is a desirable direction for you.

It is of utmost importance for the free soul that every man spend some time in solitude, getting acquainted with his own inner being. "It is very dissipating," says Thoreau, "to be with people too much. God is alone, but the Devil has a lot of company." Since the majority is as likely to be wrong as right, you must be indifferent to its praise as well as its censure. "I would rather hear a single shrub oak leaf at the end of a wintry glade rustle of its own accord at my approach than receive a shipload of stars and garters from the strange kings and people of the earth."

Thoreau believed in the direct approach. Go to headquarters for information. The simplest and plainest rule of conduct is always the best. When he wanted a boat, he built one. When he wanted a hut in which to live in the woods, he spent no time wishing that some miracle would bring it into being; he went and built that, too. When it occurred to him that it would be pleasant to go and visit Canada, he promptly went, shutting the door of his hut against possible rain, but not locking it against possible thieves.

No sooner had the suggestion been made (by Emerson) that he keep a journal than he instantly began to do so, writing in it almost every day for the rest of his life, and building thereby the whole of his worldwide fame, since all his books were carved out of this daily record.

Walking by a river on a hot day, he wanted to bathe but had no bathing suit. He therefore stripped off his clothes, all but his straw hat, and, immersed in the water up to his neck, strolled along the riverbed, stopping frequently to study the teeming life, animal and vegetable, in the stream, on its floor, and along the banks.

It was tragic, he felt, that people modify their

ambitions with passing years. "The youth gets together his materials to build a bridge to the moon . . . and at length the middle-aged man concludes to build a woodshed with them." Stick to your guns no matter how many people call you wrong. "Say, Not so, and you will outcircle the philosophers." "It is our souls that rust in a corner," he observed. "Let us migrate interiorly without intermission."

All his life, Thoreau poured out his scorn for those who are ruled by things. "Many a poor immortal soul," he wrote, "have I met well-nigh crushed and smothered under its load, creeping down the road of life, pushing before it a barn . . . and one hundred acres of land, tillage, mowing, pasture and woodlot." He insisted, indeed, that "most of the luxuries and many of the so-called comforts of life are not only not indispensable, but positive hindrances to the elevation of mankind. Our life is frittered away by detail; simplify, simplify!"

When he lived at Walden he reported, "I had three pieces of limestone on my desk, but I was terrified to find that they required to be dusted daily, when the furniture of my mind was all undusted still, and I threw them out the window in disgust."

He objected to too much emphasis on how one looks. "Beware of all enterprises that require new clothes. There is greater anxiety, commonly, to have fashionable, or at least, clean and unpatched, clothes, than to have a sound conscience." Travelers should be careful not to dress too well, or strangers will fear to make friends with them.

Thoreau's greatest impact on subsequent generations has beyond doubt been his insistence that you should do what seems best to you, scorning the opinion of others, even if this means defying a government you believe to be in the wrong. "If [injustice] is of such a nature that it requires you to be the agent of injustice to another," he observes sternly, "then I say break the law." He scorned those who thought they had done their whole duty when they voted properly. "Voting for the right is doing nothing for it. It is only expressing to men feebly your desire that it should prevail." Even the famous democratic doctrine of majority rule did not escape his scalpel: "Any man more right than his neighbors constitutes a majority of one already." This could of course be dangerous doctrine in the hands of one less pure of heart than Thoreau, but he felt the risk must be taken. No one really knows you but yourself. "What a man thinks of himself, that it is which determines . . . his fate." "However mean your life is, meet it and live it; do not shun it and call it hard names."

With so many wonderful things to do and see and think about, in the world, Thoreau was impatient with those who are ever content with less than the best. He said he subscribed to a newspaper only because it was good to wrap bundles or start fires (though as a very young man spending a few months on Staten Island, and homesick, he had sung a different tune). "If we read of one man robbed, or murdered, or killed by accident," he argued, "or one house burned, or one vessel cracked, or one steamboat blown up, or one cow run over on the Western Railroad, or one mad dog killed, or one lot of grasshoppers in the winter—

we never need read of another. One is enough. If you are acquainted with the principle, what do you care for a myriad instances and applications?"

It was on this basis that he urged we should read the best books first, lest by delay we never get a chance to read them at all. He noticed wryly, however, that you could always start a conversation if you had just perused the latest popular novel, while everyone remained silent if you mentioned something you had just found in a Greek philosopher.

A thousand men have paraphrased without realizing the source, his comment that "we are in great haste to construct a magnetic telegraph from Maine to Texas; but Maine and Texas, it may be, have nothing important to communicate." Exaggerating to prove his point, he wrote that "as for England, almost the last significant scrap of news from that quarter was the Revolution of 1649"—two hundred years earlier.

Thoreau believed that man can only be happy when he surrenders himself to the harmony of Nature. "To be serene and successful we must be at one with the universe . . . It is the marriage of the soul with Nature that makes the intellect fruitful, that gives birth to imagination. If a plant cannot live according to its nature it dies, and so does a man." He contrasted natural freedom with the inhibitions men impose upon themselves: "He is constraint, [Nature] is freedom. The joy which Nature yields is like that afforded by the frank words of one we love. Pile up your books, the records of sadness, your saws [wise sayings] and your laws. Nature is glad outside, and her merry worms within will ere long topple them down." The poet knows these truths instinctively, the pedant never. "It is only when we forget all our learning that we begin to know. Poetry cannot breathe in the scholar's atmosphere . . . We can never have enough of Nature. The earth I tread on is a body, has a spirit, is organic."

Thoreau's writings are shot through with love, first of Nature, and then of his fellowman. In passages of unequaled lyric beauty he described the wilderness and its inhabitants, while behind his often gruff and forbidding exterior, he had also an abiding love for humanity. He shared his small amounts of money, and even his possessions, with the desperately poor Irish immigrants of the neighborhood; he went from door to door among the prosperous Yankees, trying to raise money to help a family in great need—and reported the ready excuses made by most to justify a refusal.

"The only way to speak the truth," he wrote, "is to speak lovingly; only the lover's words are heard. The intellect should never speak; it is not a natural sound." Indeed, you cannot really succeed in anything unless you love, and are happy in, your occupation. "It is always essential that we love to do what we are doing, do it with a heart. I can express adequately only the thought which I *love* to express."

He also recognized that anyone who offers love to the world is in danger of being misunderstood. "If Christ should appear on earth, he would on all hands be denounced as a mistaken, misguided man."

Thoreau died much too young, at the age of forty-five; his constitution had been weakened by earlier attacks of the great scourge of his day, tuberculosis. When he was on his deathbed, his Aunt Louisa asked him whether he "had made his peace with God." His characteristic reply was, "I did not know that we had ever quarreled, Aunt."

While it is true that his reputation, such a towering oak today, was then only a tender green shoot, a few recognized his genius. A Boston paper commented, "When we now look back at the solitude of his erect and spotless person, we lament that he did not live long enough for all men to know him." Ralph Waldo Emerson, who spoke at his funeral service, gave him the final yet prophetic tribute: "The country knows not yet, or in the least part, how great a man it has lost . . . Wherever there is knowledge, wherever there is virtue, wherever there is beauty, he will find a home."

Epilogue

Epilogue: The Measure of Greatness

NOBODY HAS EVER, so far as I know, given an adequate definition of the complex of characteristics we call greatness, and I shall certainly not be so presumptuous as to try. Its qualities are surely as rich and varied as the personalities of the six individuals in this book. It would in any case be absurd to try to generalize on the basis of these six persons—or sixty.

If we do not know what greatness is, we can list a few things that it is not. First of all, it is not charisma; many outstanding individuals have had none, and history is full of charming scoundrels. It is not necessarily very high intelligence, as measured on the I.Q. scale; some of the greatest men and women have been noted for character rather than mental resources. And it is not the judgment of one's contemporaries, which is as likely to be wrong as right. The three subjects of greatest popular adulation in this century among native-born Americans have been Adm. George Dewey, Col. Charles Lindbergh, and, for a few years in his youth, Frank Sinatra.

There seems to be an inverse ratio between the number of great individuals who are identified as such, and the size of the population. In 1775, on the eve of the American Revolution, that of the United States was presumably not more than three million. Of that number, all the evidence we have suggests that only a small handful, perhaps a few hundred, had the personality, long-continued achievements, and the other attributes to make them highly distinguished, the sort of individual who is without cavil described as great.

In 1860, just before the Civil War, the population had grown about ten times. I doubt whether any historian would claim that the number who would qualify for this description was ten times larger. And the disproportion in the 1970s, when the population is about seventy times as great as in 1775, must certainly be very much bigger still.

To come down from the generality of mankind to

the few—a hard transition—this book is mainly concerned with the lives of six people under great stress —the sort of stress that, by the grim Darwinian doctrine of the survival of the fittest, often destroys lesser individuals. Yet it is worth giving at least a passing glance to the factors in their lives that are commonly assumed to fit an individual to triumph over, as Tom Paine said, "the times that try men's souls," beginning, inevitably, with their ancestry.

Of the twelve parents, only one came from a really notable line: Jefferson's mother was one of the famous Randolph family of Virginia. (It is true, of course, that some of the other individuals may have had remarkable gifts which for some reason or another never saw the light of day.)

Franklin's father was an immigrant from England, where the family had for three hundred years been small farmers and blacksmiths. His mother's family was equally undistinguished, though his maternal grandfather was a writer in a modest way, the author of tracts attacking the persecution of the Quakers and Baptists in New England. His father, after arriving in America, became a tallow merchant and candlemaker.

John Adams came from a series of small landholders; like Franklin's family, they had been farmers in England. John, who founded such a remarkable dynasty of writers and political figures, was the fifth generation in America, with no notable personalities recorded in either the father's or the mother's family.

Jefferson's paternal ancestors were cast in a similar mold, with no outstanding individuals so far as history reveals. However, his father was a landholder and surveyor, justice of the peace, a colonel in the county militia, and a burgess.

Sojourner Truth's parents were slaves, who had almost no chance to show whatever abilities they possessed, though they seem to have been good people. Of her ancestors beyond her mother's mother, we know nothing.

Emerson came from six generations of New England ministers, worthy but not outstanding individuals, always living in genteel poverty. His father died when Ralph was eight, and responsibilities were thrust upon the boy early.

Thoreau was the grandson of an immigrant from the Channel Islands. His father was almost a ne'er-do-well, who failed at various things until he set up a cottage industry making pencils, an occupation in which Thoreau himself worked half-heartedly for many years.

Not much is known about the mothers of these six individuals. Our only knowledge of Sojourner's mother comes from the daughter's memories, dictated many years later to Olive Gilbert. As for the mothers of the five men on my list, in the eighteenth century, and even in the middle of the nineteenth, a wife and mother was supposed to subordinate herself to her husband and her children, and unless she was a very strong character indeed, she did. None of the five mothers seems to have been conspicuously above or below the average. Large families were the rule: Franklin, as the eighth of ten children of his father's second wife, was not an exceptional case. Housekeeping was far more onerous than it is today, except for the rich who could afford several servants—true only of the family of Jefferson.

When we consider physical health, a matter usually supposed to be important for great achievement, the record is again a mixed one. Franklin was a remarkable athlete as a young man, a noted long-distance swimmer. Adams was a hypochondriac, but the record he set of tremendous bouts of hard work is inconsistent with frail health. Jefferson, also, showed much endurance. He and Adams were both great walkers, and also ardent horsemen, spending many hours in the saddle.

Sojourner had much strength and endurance, or she could never have survived the cruelties of her early years, and her health seems to have been good until the very last years of her life.

Emerson as a young man had bad eyes and "weak lungs," being sent to Florida for this reason; the incidence of tuberculosis in New England in the mid-nineteenth century was very heavy. But in later life he seemed sturdy. He was a sedentary man, but he endured serious hardships on his long lecture tours, and like all the other men in this book, except Thoreau, turned out an enormous volume of work. He lived to be seventy-nine, a good age for that era, or our own.

It was tuberculosis that killed Thoreau, at the young age of forty-five. But in spite of his handicap, he always worked hard when he worked. He also took long walks every day, summer or winter, and set such a pace that many who tried to accompany him complained. As noted, he was not notoriously diligent—except in pursuit of his own special interests—and thus differed from the other men I have discussed, but this was more for philosophical than physical reasons. He thought most of the things most men did were not worth doing.

The three eighteenth-century men all crossed the ocean when to do so was a severe physical ordeal; the sailing ships were small, accommodations cramped, the voyages were long, and death at sea was not at all uncommon. The fact that Adams, Franklin, and Jefferson survived these voyages is a tribute to their physical endurance.

Perhaps the only generalization we can make about the health of these six individuals is that all of them had abounding vitality most of the time, an avid interest in life, and, except for periods of depression, confidence in their ability to meet its problems head on.

When we consider their childhood experiences, it is again difficult to draw firm conclusions. Franklin always felt he had been misused by his family, and perhaps he was, though poverty may have been more to blame than ill will. He resented being apprenticed to his brother at the age of twelve, and finally ran away to Philadelphia, but we cannot now judge whether the rigors of his childhood and youth did him harm or stimulated him to achievement.

John Adams was also rebellious against home discipline. He had an abrasive temperament; perhaps if we could hear his parents' side of the story we might feel that both were at fault. The home conflicts seem to have abated when he went to Harvard.

Jefferson appears to have had an average childhood for his time and place, until the death of his father when he was fourteen. After his two years at William and Mary College, he studied law for five years, being admitted to the bar at the age of twenty-four. His wide-ranging interests are evidenced by his learning Latin, Greek, French, Spanish, Italian, calculus, and natural science.

Sojourner's childhood seems to us today one unrelieved horror. But between the climaxes of terror and despair, it may not have seemed quite as bad to her. Most of the other slaves she knew had treatment as bad as hers, and sometimes worse.

Emerson had a normal childhood, as far as the record shows, at least until his father died when he was eight. His life was hard, because of poverty, but there is no evidence that the privations hurt him, and they may have helped.

Thoreau was a rebel all his life; we don't know very much about his childhood except that he was poor, and had to work at various parental projects before he was adolescent. (So did all but one of the others in this book.) He was not an enthusiastic scholar at Harvard; it was Emerson, in the years after graduation, who stimulated his intellectual growth.

When we consider the marital status of my protagonists, the record is inconclusive. Sojourner's marriage, of course, had nothing to do with her career; it was over, for all practical purposes, before her remarkable metamorphosis. As to the five men, the evidence as to whether their wives helped or hindered is in most cases not clear. All but Thoreau married, and Emerson twice, but the only wife who seems to have been a remarkable, strong personality was Abigail Adams.

Franklin's common-law wife, Deborah, was a good manager of his household, but no match for him intellectually. She died in 1774, on the eve of the great events of Revolution; during Franklin's long service in Paris he was a widower. But all his life he had sought close ties with other women, some of whom provided the intellectual stimulus Deborah never was able to give.

Jefferson's wife, who died after only ten years of marriage, was competent in household affairs, but apparently not an outstanding intellect in her own right. He loved her dearly, and her death was a profound shock from which it took him a long time to recover.

Emerson's second wife followed the pattern of the times; she let her husband have the limelight while she looked after his physical well-being. She exerted real influence upon the young Thoreau, so long a member of the Emerson ménage; as noted, some people believe he was secretly in love with her. His other, acknowledged, love affair sounds like a story Eugene O'Neill might have invented—the discovery that his brother was in love with the same girl, his brother's death, and then after he himself had been accepted, the action of his fiancée's father in breaking up the romance. But there is no evidence I can discover that his love affairs had any strong influence on his career, for good or bad.

When we come to consider the general environmental factors in the lives of my six protagonists, we see a common pattern in the lives of most of them. Sojourner's whole life, except for the last few years, was lived among difficulties and dangers equaled only part of the time by the three men of the Revolution, and by the second two in this book hardly at all, though four were brought up in real poverty.

All of them but Franklin grew up under the shadow of an impending, terrible war. In 1776, when the Revolution started in earnest, Adams was forty-one, Jefferson thirty-three; only Franklin was an old man of seventy. For Jefferson and Adams, the mistreatment of the colonies by the British government was certainly the great overshadowing fact of their young lives. Even to Franklin, immersed as he was as a newspaper editor in national and international affairs, the coming storm was apparent for many years before it broke. For men like Adams and Jefferson, growing up under these circumstances must have been an element of great discipline and character formation.

When the Civil War broke out in 1861, Sojourner was sixty-four, Emerson fifty-eight, Thoreau forty-four. But as in the case of the eighteenth-century men, coming events cast a long shadow forward over their times. Years before the war began, Emerson and Thoreau, and Sojourner most of all, were caught up in the antislavery issue and the activities of the Underground Railroad. (Thoreau, younger than Emerson, came to the movement earlier and was more ardent in its support.)

The overt acts preceding the Revolution took ten years, from the Stamp Act in 1765 to Lexington and Concord, and Bunker Hill, in 1775. When it came, it was the most desperate of forlorn hopes. Only half the people of the colonies sympathized with the rebels; they had no real army, no navy, no munitions, no money, and only a skeleton government, the Continental Congress, formed on the very eve of the outbreak of hostilities. But to Adams and Jefferson, brought up as they had been, participation in the conflict was inevitable; and it was equally so to old Ben Franklin. Their characters had been hardened in the fire of the long struggle with the British King, and needed no more tempering in the bitter hardships of the dragged-out quarrel that was to follow.

When the Civil War began in 1861, Sojourner sent a grandson. Emerson at fifty-eight was too old to fight. Thoreau was forty-four, with only one more year to live. (He would have been rejected for the armed forces on medical grounds, and spiritually, few have ever lived who resisted external discipline so strongly.) Of the five men in this book the first three were political figures; an active role in the conflict their country faced was inevitable. The other two were writers and thinkers, not men of action. Yet there is no doubt that Emerson and Thoreau were shaped in varying ways and degrees by the times through which they lived.

When we come to discuss their personal characteristics, we note that the five educated individuals were enormously addicted to reading, the first three perhaps even more than the other two. In the middle of the eighteenth century, books were scarce and expensive, which made them doubly treasured; a hundred years later, they were numerous, but still not so readily available as they are to most Americans today.

Any reader of my pages must agree that Sojourner had a remarkable power of expression; if she had been able to write, I think she would have been successful. The five men were all, of course, gifted authors; every one of them produced books that had a great effect upon their readers (though Thoreau's influence was delayed by some decades). Franklin was the first popular journalist in America. Adams and Jefferson wrote primarily tracts for their times, seeking to change conditions, or to support changes already in progress. Emerson and Thoreau were professional essayists more than anything else.

The three eighteenth-century men sought to influence the citizenry directly, and succeeded; Emerson and Thoreau wrote primarily for an elite of the intellect. Sojourner, in her hundreds of speeches, was a passionate advocate of great human causes. Emerson, the cool and academic scholar, helped set the minds of other scholars free from parochialism, and probed the depths of the human spirit as few have ever done. Thoreau, in rebellion against nearly everything in our civilization, wrote partly as a naturalist, partly to persuade others to see what he saw, and partly to record his own grievances.

At least in political life, it is essential that an outstanding individual should be able to work well in harness with others. Adams, in spite of his sharp tongue and his sometimes too patent egoism, generally got on well with committees and other groups; he conducted successful negotiations on behalf of his government with several European countries. Franklin succeeded even better than Adams with the people he met, of every station in life. Jefferson made a great point of being affable to strangers; he was always picking them up along the road to ride with him in his coach, or striking up conversations in taverns. But he seems to have been by nature a little withdrawn, and to have assumed a geniality not quite innate. Sojourner made lifelong friends of nearly everyone she met, except those so bitterly opposed to her causes that they could not approach her with an open mind.

Emerson, like Jefferson, sought out people to find out how they lived and what they thought, but there was a touch of the sociologist in all this; at heart he was a cloistered scholar. Thoreau was a loner; he got on fairly well with the people of Concord, considering that they thought him a very odd duck indeed, but he was a type who clung closely to a few friends, and did not need a host of acquaintances.

Only one of these six individuals made money, or showed any interest in doing so. Franklin had a substantial fortune, by the standards of the day, when he retired from the publishing business to devote the rest of his life, so he erroneously thought, largely to science. Adams and his family lived mainly on salaries, never enough. Jefferson started with a modest inheritance, but spent nearly all his days harassed by debt. Sojourner was poor, as to material things, all her life. Emerson had barely enough money to be able to help Thoreau and that chronic indigent, Bronson Alcott. Thoreau lived his short span on a handyman's wages, or less.

Adams complained of not having enough, but Adams complained about everything. Franklin, who began with less than any of the others including Thoreau, was money-minded as a young man, not as an old one. In general, none of them cared for money as much as they did for other things which were the main preoccupation of their lives.

While as I have said, we cannot generalize about greatness from the example of a few, it is true that these six people did have characteristics and experiences in common that we know to have been shared by large numbers of others, throughout history. It seems clear that for true greatness, you need intelligence, which is an inborn characteristic, and strength of character, which usually comes with rearing. An exceptional degree of the second of these can sometimes compensate for a lesser degree of the other, as many instances demonstrate.

History proves, it seems to me, that for outstanding achievement, the environment must make heavy demands—but not too heavy—upon the individual, even in childhood. The brain is like the muscles; it is strengthened by exercise, and tends to grow flabby with disuse. This does not necessarily mean that parents must be strict, or schoolwork wearisome; the child can be spurred on by other factors.

In adult life, the environment must also be in some way demanding. In the case of one with a talent for music or painting or authorship, this means a milieu in which achievement in these fields is recognized and rewarded. In the case of public affairs, I should say that something must be seriously wrong which is capable of being remedied. If reform is hopeless, apathy is the almost inevitable result, even though there are always a few who will keep on trying against impossible odds.

Are conditions as favorable in America today to the

creation of greatness as they were one hundred or two hundred years ago? This is an enormously complicated question to which there is no easy and simple answer. The problems by which we are faced today as a nation are certainly as difficult as any ever encountered in the past, involving as they do the question whether mankind itself can survive. But they are so complex that many are in despair; the questions Americans had to solve in the past now seem naively simple by comparison—though not to those struggling with them at the time!

Sociologists nowadays believe that there is a limit to the possible growth of any community, beyond which it becomes so diffuse and amorphous that the individual tends to get lost in the crowd. Some think that in cities, this number may in the past have been as low as one hundred thousand; the Athens of twenty-five hundred years ago, with the most extraordinary assembly of highly gifted individuals in all history, had only about fifty thousand free citizens. The "spiritual size" of the group shrinks in time of war, or any other great national peril. It is also possible, of course, that modern means of communication, and especially television, may be reducing the community again.

The lives of middle-class white Americans were certainly soft much of the time in the late middle decades of the twentieth century. It is commonly said that the children of this group, brought up in affluence, are spoiled by it. But there is little complacency among a large proportion of blacks and other minorities, and even among some members of the majority which thinks of itself as a minority: women. If adversity is a necessary ingredient for distinction, it is perhaps to these groups that we should in the future look for examples of individual achievement.

Emerson and Thoreau were talented writers; they could have applied their talents ably in any age, and Thoreau in particular might have been more successful in the day of the counterculture than he was in his own. Franklin would certainly be an enormously successful practitioner of one or another of the arts of mass communication. Adams and Jefferson would have applied themselves to the national problems of any age. If Sojourner had had the education appropriate to her abilities, and had not suffered the fearful handicap of the color bar (existing today as it did for her), there is no telling what she might have accomplished.

There is a fatal flaw in the question, What would these individuals do if they lived today? because in a new time they would not have been the same. We are all the product of the immediate society in which we are bred; Franklin or Jefferson, born in the twentieth century, would not be Franklin or Jefferson, but someone else. As the writer has finally concluded (and as the reader doubtless knew all the time!) we shall do best if we content ourselves with looking back with pleasure at the magnificent lives those individuals led, and the heritage they have left us.

About the Author

BRUCE BLIVEN is a graduate of Stanford University, and a former head of the Department of Journalism at the University of Southern California. He has spent most of his life in journalism, having been a member of the staff of *The San Francisco Bulletin,* that of *Printers' Ink,* and managing editor of the (daily) *New York Globe.* He spent thirty years on *The New Republic,* half that time as editor. For twenty years he was New York correspondent for the British daily, *The Guardian,* then called *The Manchester Guardian.* He has written five books, was editor of two others, has taught part-time at New York University, Columbia, and Stanford, has lectured in many cities in the United States, and has contributed to numerous magazines. He now lives with his wife at Stanford.